The New York Times

CHANGING PERSPECTIVES

Gun Control

THE NEW YORK TIMES EDITORIAL STAFF

Published in 2019 by The New York Times® Educational Publishing
in association with The Rosen Publishing Group, Inc.
29 East 21st Street, New York, NY 10010

First Edition

The New York Times
Alex Ward: Editorial Director, Book Development
Phyllis Collazo: Photo Rights/Permissions Editor
Heidi Giovine: Administrative Manager

Rosen Publishing
Megan Kellerman: Managing Editor
Elizabeth Schmermund: Editor
Greg Tucker: Creative Director
Brian Garvey: Art Director

Cataloging-in-Publication Data
Names: New York Times Company.
Title: Gun control / edited by the New York Times editorial staff.
Description: New York : New York Times Educational Publishing,
2019. | Series: Changing perspectives | Includes glossary and index.
Identifiers: ISBN 9781642821468 (library bound) | ISBN
9781642821451 (pbk.) | ISBN 9781642821475 (ebook)
Subjects: LCSH: Gun control—Juvenile literature. | Gun control—
United States—Juvenile literature.
Classification: LCC HV7435.G86 2019 | DDC 363.330973—dc23

Manufactured in the United States of America

On the cover: A close-up of Jeff Nass, president of WI-FORCE, a
gun rights group in Wis.; Narayan Mahon for The New York Times.

Contents

CHAPTER 2

The Reagan Years and Shifts in Gun Laws

CHAPTER 3

A Call for Greater Gun Control

Introduction

FOR MANY, GUNS are inextricably linked to both the history of the United States and the contemporary moment. Guns were an integral part of both our nation's independence from Great Britain in the 18th century and the expansion of the western frontier in the 19th century. Those who believe that guns should not be regulated often cite the Second Amendment of our Constitution, which states, "A well regulated Militia, being necessary to the security of a free State, the right of the people to keep and bear Arms, shall not be infringed." Advocates of gun control, however, see the Second Amendment as a historical document that must be reinterpreted in our contemporary moment; they believe that, for the Founding Fathers, a "well regulated" militia was essential to gaining independence and becoming a new nation, but it is less important today.

But times have certainly changed. While violence has always — unfortunately — played a large role in human societies, mass shootings have occurred more frequently in recent decades and have received more media attention. The definitions of a mass shooting differ, but it is generally considered to be the indiscriminate shooting and death of four or more people, not related to gang activity, other crimes or military action. In the United States, mass shootings were not part of broad public attention until Charles Whitman shot his wife and mother and then killed fourteen people from the clock tower at the University of Texas at Austin in 1966.

The 1960s also brought the assassinations of many high-profile political and civil rights figures, including John F. Kennedy, Malcolm X, Martin Luther King Jr. and Robert Kennedy, among many others. During this period of time, gun control measures were introduced in Congress and then blocked, largely through the lobbying of the National Rifle Association (N.R.A.). Although the N.R.A., which advocates for gun rights, has been in existence since 1871, it first began to lobby effectively against gun restrictions in the late 1960s and 1970s. The issue of gun control during this time was also inextricably linked with the civil rights movement — and with racism. Gun rights advocates often stated that widespread gun ownership would help protect white people from attacks by other races, while those who were pro-gun-control argued that gun restrictions would keep guns out of the hands of black power groups like the Black Panthers. Unfortunately, the gun control debates of the 1960s and 1970s were largely steeped in bigoted and racist ideology.

The issue of gun control has been no less complex in the years since. Like the attack at the University of Texas in 1966, the 1999 school shooting at Columbine High School, in Colorado, became a watershed moment. Thirteen students and teachers were killed that day, and the

People in Chicago gather to remember the victims of a shooting spree in Las Vegas in October 2017 and to advocate for stricter gun control. More than 500 people were injured and 59 people were killed, making it the deadliest mass shooting up to that point.

nation broke out in fevered debate about the role of gun laws, bullying and mental health in such deadly attacks.

Since then, school shootings seem to have become a much more common occurrence in the United States. From the 2012 attack on Sandy Hook Elementary School in Connecticut to the 2018 Santa Fe High School shooting in Texas, it appears as if we have reached a tipping point in terms of gun violence and schools. In particular, younger generations who are fatigued by the emotional stress of school shootings — or who have lost loved ones in these attacks — have begun to organize and speak out for greater gun control in the United States. They have experienced great resistance from the N.R.A. as well as from Republicans in Congress. However, this might be changing. With mass shootings almost becoming commonplace in the United States, more voices are speaking out for common-sense measures, such as a national registry of gun owners or mental health background checks. For advocates of gun control, the path appears rocky and long — after all, gun control measures have been introduced and defeated in the U.S. Congress for over fifty years — but there is reason to hope that change is nigh.

CHAPTER 1

Early Gun Control Measures

Gun control issues began to receive more widespread attention in the U.S. media in the 1960s. Despite a series of assassinations — President John F. Kennedy in November 1963, Malcolm X in February 1965, Martin Luther King Jr. in April 1968 and Robert Kennedy in June 1968 — many gun control efforts languished in Congress. The National Rifle Association, a gun-rights group, developed into a powerful voice against gun control during this period. However, the 1968 Gun Control Act, which regulated interstate traffic of firearms, was passed despite the group's objections.

Gun-Curbs Issue Revived by Dodd

BY BEN A. FRANKLIN | JAN. 17, 1965

WASHINGTON, JAN. 16 — The prospects for success of a renewed Congressional drive to restrict and control the growing mail-order trade in cheap guns have been enhanced this year.

The expected support of the Johnson Administration for firearms control legislation and the compliant attitude of the overwhelmingly Democratic congress are major factors, observers here believe.

The opposition to any gun controls has also grown. Although restrictions on mail-order guns are supported by the biggest and most influential shooters' organization, the National Rifle Association, there are 15 million to 20 million hunters and gun enthusiasts in the country who are not affiliated with it.

Moreover, many association gun clubs disagree bitterly with their national organization on the issue. Together, the opposition to gun curbs is formidable and vocal.

The measure that is expected to be the focus of controversy is the Dodd bill, introduced as S. 14 by Senator Thomas J. Dodd, Democrat of Connecticut, with 10 co-sponsors. An identical bill, H. R. 1539, was offered in the House of Representatives by Edward A. Garmatz, Democrat of Maryland.

A similar bill died last year in the Senate Commerce Committee, whose chairman, Senator Warren G. Magnuson of Washington, is strongly opposed to Federal gun control legislation. Mr. Magnuson has acknowledged the problem of proliferating mail-order bargain weapons, but he believes controls should be exercised by the states.

In the House, Mr. Garmatz's bill has been referred to the Ways and Means Committee.

The Dodd bill is aimed specifically at the growing mail-order trade in the cheap, war surplus arms of foreign countries. These are imported in large numbers at very low cost and retailed at $5, $10, or $20 usually without any examination by the purchaser. The profit mark-up is attractive.

Mr. Dodd, the Warren Commission and others have had little difficulty in dramatizing the distribution of such weapons. President Kennedy's assassin, Lee Harvey Oswald, obtained his Mannlicher-Carcano 6.5-mm. rifle, an Italian military castoff, for $21.45, including a four-power telescopic sight. The Chicago mail-order house that sold it offered the same rifle without a scope at $12.78.

The Oswald rifle was shipped to Dallas under the assassin's alias, A. Hidell, with no questions asked.

The Dodd bill would require mail-order dealers to withhold such a shipment unless the order was accompanied by a signed statement that the buyer was 21 or over, in compliance with local, state, and Federal firearms regulations, and not a convicted felon, a habitual drunkard or a narcotics addict.

The significance of this statement is that the dealer would then be required, under the law, to forward it to the police authorities in the purchaser's jurisdiction. This, it is thought, would provide local law-enforcement agencies with the information that the firearm had been shipped. This provision would apply to the interstate shipment of rifles, shotguns and handguns.

MILDER BILL IS OFFERED

A stronger version of this process, in which a gun dealer would have been required to await the mailed approval of the local police chief before making shipment, was dropped from the bill last year as unworkable and as probably unconstitutional.

As revised, the Dodd bill is considered even milder than last year's version. New language has been inserted removing the affidavit and notification procedures in the shipment of privately owned guns for servicing by gunsmiths, a step that was considered an unnecessary nuisance to gun owners.

Nonetheless, resistance to the bill is expected to be even stronger than last year, when Mr. Dodd charged that "hysterical opposition" had caused the measure to be pigeonholed in committee.

Franklin L. Orth, executive vice president of the N.R.A., said today that the organization's executive committee had given him "full authority to go ahead with support of the bill."

"It is a tough position for us to take in this highly emotionalized atmosphere," he said.

Mr. Orth has called for N.R.A. membership support of the Dodd bill as a "sensible measure" that will "protect the sport of shooting from sweeping proposals to ban guns altogether."

Mr. Dodd is expected to use his chairmanship of a Senate subcommittee on juvenile delinquency to dramatize other areas of alleged firearms abuse.

There have been persistent reports that a few paramilitary extremist groups have armed themselves with heavy field weapons.

Mr. Dodd's subcommittee may examine these reports, thus giving impetus to the mail-order legislation by exposing abuses.

Another Dodd proposal would sharply restrict or possibly prohibit the importation of virtually all foreign surplus weapons. This proposal has been favored by Senator Robert F. Kennedy, Democrat of New York.

Drop That Gun

EDITORIAL | BY THE NEW YORK TIMES | MAY 24, 1965

THE ADMINISTRATION'S gun-control bill, which is now the subject of Senate hearings, is excellent as far as it goes, but it does not go far enough. The bill would ban the sale of guns through the mails, would increase license fees for gun dealers and, except for certain kinds of hunting rifles, would forbid the sale of firearms to persons under 21.

Senator Robert P. Kennedy has made an additional — and desirable — proposal. Since private citizens have no legitimate use for antitank guns, mortars and machine guns, the sale or possession of such heavy weapons should be forbidden by law. We sympathize with Mr. Kennedy's further suggestion that such groups as the Minute Men and the Ku Klux Klan be stripped of their private arsenals; but it is doubtful such a law could be drafted without infringing on the activities of legitimate sportsmen's clubs.

There is another aspect of the problem that has received less attention than it deserves. Many cheap foreign weapons have been imported in recent years and are today in the hands of licensed dealers — so many that some kind of domestic arms control and disarmament program is in order. Government purchase of these stocks of surplus guns, in order to destroy them, would be money well spent.

Attorney General Katzenbach has testified that cities which have strict gun-control regulations have substantially lower rates of homicides committed with guns than do cities without such regulations. Homicides committed with guns in Dallas and Phoenix, for example, occur at a rate two to three times as great as in New York and Philadelphia.

In short, laws do make a difference, and it is time the nation had a much stricter law to diminish and supervise the traffic in guns.

President Asserts Texas
Shooting Points Up Need for a Law

BY ROBERT B. SEMPLE JR. | AUG. 3, 1966

WASHINGTON, AUG. 2 — President Johnson, deploring yesterday's mass killings at the University of Texas, today urged prompt enactment of gun control legislation now stalled in Congress.

In a statement read to newsmen by Bill D. Moyers, his press secretary, Mr. Johnson declared:

"The shocking tragedy of yesterday's events in Austin is heightened because they were senseless. While senseless, however, what happened is not without a lesson: That we must press urgently for the legislation now pending in Congress to help prevent the wrong persons from obtaining firearms.

"The bill would not prevent all such tragedies; but it would help reduce the unrestricted sale of firearms to those who cannot be trusted in their use or possession. How many lives might be saved as a consequence?

"The gun control bill has been under consideration in the Congress for many months. The time has come for action."

Mr. Johnson said there were many in Congress who shared his views and he urged then "to join in passing this legislation."

The President, according to aides, was profoundly saddened by yesterday's incident, which saw Charles J. Whitman, a 25-year-old architectural student, kill 12 persons, and wound 3 others during an hour and a half of sniping from the top of the Univerity of Texas tower. Earlier he had killed his wife and mother. Whitman's arsenal included three rifles, a shotgun, two pistols, and a knife.

Among those killed was Paul Sonntag, an 18-year-old University student and grandson of Paul Bolton, a news executive for KTBC-AM-TV, the broad casting outlet of the Texas Broadcasting Company in Austin, which is owned by the Johnson family. The President

Police speak at a press conference after Charles Whitman's sniper attack at the University of Texas at Austin.

and Mrs. Johnson telephoned their condolences to Mr. Bolton last evening.

The President also sent a message of sympathy to the chancellor of the University of Texas, Harry Hansom. "Mrs. Johnson and I know the heavy burden so many are bearing as a result of the tragedy yesterday," Mr. Johnson's message said. "We are deeply grieved, and our hearts go out to the families involved and to all who are suffering. We want to assure you of any personal or official assistance that would in any way be helpful."

STRONGEST ENDORSEMENT

The President's statement on gun-control legislation — which constituted the strongest public endorsement he has given to the legislation — was accompanied by widespread demands in Congress for prompt acceptance of laws restricting the sale and use of firearms.

But despite hopes that the Austin killings would spur action, observers here were cautious about predicting final success for a gun control bill.

They recalled that after the assassination of President Kennedy in November, 1963, there was a strong drive for passage for restrictive measures. However, the drive collapsed before the powerful opposition of the National Rifle Association and other gun clubs.

At present, gun control legislation is pending in slightly different form in both houses. In the Senate, an Administration-backed measure, whose chief sponsor is Thomas J. Dodd, Democrat of Connecticut, was approved last March 22 by a subcommittee of the Senate Judiciary Committee.

The legislation is now on the agenda of the full Judiciary Committee but there is no indication of when it will come up for a vote. Even if the bill receives the committee's approval, it must then confront the Senate Commerce Committee, where a majority is said to oppose the bill.

In its major provisions, the Dodd bill would:

• Ban the interstate mail order sale of concealable firearms — such as pistols and revolvers — to all individuals.

• Regulate the interstate sale of sporting rifles and shotguns through an affidavit provision;

• Restrict the importation of surplus military arms and certain other foreign-made firearms;

• Bar the sale of pistols and revolvers to persons under 21;

• Ban the over-the-counter sale of concealable firearms to persons who are not residents of the state wherein the licensee — the dealer — does his business.

Asked how his bill could have, prevented yesterday's tragedy, Mr. Dodd replied: "I've never claimed that if the bill was passed it would put an end to all murders by firearms. But it would be a deterrent. If it had been passed, the retailer who sold Charles Whitman the gun yesterday would have had to get positive identification."

The bill's affidavit provision requires that purchasers of rifles and shotguns sign an affidavit disclosing their identity, address, and felony record, if any. Even though Whitman did not have such a record, Mr. Dodd suggested that the mere fact of having to identify himself may have caused him to hesitate and perhaps interrupted his plans for the mass homicide.

Mr. Dodd also promised to try to amend the legislation in full committee to ban the interstate sale of rifles and shotguns, in addition to concealable weapons. Earlier efforts by the Senator to include such a provision were rebuffed by the subcommittee last March. At his news briefing this morning, Mr. Moyers said flatly that the White House would support any effort to broaden the bill to cover long arms.

The stiffest opposition to the bill has come from the National Rifle Association, an organization with a membership of about 720,000. The association supported, in 1963 and 1964, earlier Dodd bills, which would have banned only small, concealable weapons. But their opposition to the Senator's later attempts to broaden the bill helped defeat the "long arm" provision in the Judiciary subcommittee last week.

The N.R.A. is still expected to oppose broadening the present bill despite yesterday's killings. Franklin Orth, executive vice president of the association, said today that a gun control law would not have prevented either the recent murder of eight nurses in Chicago or the slayings in Austin.

According to estimates made by the juvenile delinquency subcommittee of the Senate Judiciary committee, about a million guns were bought by mail in 1963, and that in some areas as many as 25 per cent of them were sold to convicted criminals.

The subcommittee, which conducted a two-year study of firearms traffic, also found evidence of an extraordinary correlation between areas with strict gun laws and low homicides rates.

Texas law requires only that rifles and pistols not be sold to anyone under the age of 21. Dealers are also supposed to record the name and address of purchasers of pistols and send them to the Texas Department of Public Safety.

In 1963, Dallas had a rate of 13.4 murders per 100,000 persons. New York, with the toughest weapons laws of any state in the nation, had 5.4 homicides per 100,000 population in 1963.

The new York State firearms law, known as the Sullivan Act, imposes strict regulations only on weapons such as pistols, daggers and bludgeons that can be concealed on the person.

As in other, states, the purchase of a rifle or a shotgun in New York state needs neither a permit nor regulation. Possession of machine guns and automatic rifles is illegal but semiautomatic rifles and shotguns are legal and may he maintained loaded in the home.

Carrying a loaded rifle in the city is illegal under the State Conservation Code. The discharging of rifles within the city is a misdemeanor under the Administrative Code.

The Gun and How to Control It

BY JAMES V. BENNETT | SEPT. 26, 1966

AROUND THE DOME of the nation's Capitol is a railed walkway used occasionally by painters and roofers. Should you be able to sweet-talk your way past the guards onto it, equipped with the kind of four-power Japanese scopesight used by marksmen Charles J. Whitman and Lee Harvey Oswald, you might, any Tuesday morning, be able to zero in on Senator Thomas J. Dodd some 300 yards below as he walks across the street from his office to the Senate Judiciary Committee meeting room.

His stride, you would observe, has a bit of jauntiness. That is because, after five years of investigations, hearings, reports, bills, amended bills and extended floor debates, there is some slight hope that, with the prodding of President Johnson, he may be able to get the Judiciary Committee to vote his firearms-control bill up or down. So far the committee has refused to come to grips with the issue raised by states, like New York, which demand the right to regulate who among their citizens may purchase pistols, revolvers, shotguns and other lethal weapons without having the states' efforts thwarted by out of state and mail-order sales. Though the Senator presumably has been disheartened by the committee's filibustering, he is now cheered by the belief that enough votes can be mustered with the help of an aroused public to pass the bill at the next session. Thus, after three decades of effort by nearly all law-enforcement groups — buttressed by the widespread but unorganized support of a public increasingly concerned over crime and violence — the blind and misleading opposition of a relatively small, highly organized gun lobby may be overcome.

Pending Federal proposals to curb unrestricted gun sales are simple and straightforward. The most recent Dodd bill requires anyone who wishes to buy a pistol or revolver to do so through a licensed dealer. It would no longer be possible under such a law to buy a handgun through the mails as do so many juveniles, Lee Harvey Oswalds, ex-convicts, emotionally disturbed persons or others who for one reason or another want to hide their purchases. The bill would ban over-the-counter sales of handguns to nonresidents of the dealer's state, to persons under 18, to a convicted felon or to anyone not conforming to state laws governing the purchase or ownership of guns.

The provisions with respect to buying a rifle or shotgun are less restrictive. The guns could still be bought by mail but the purchaser would need to accompany his order with an affidavit setting forth that (1) he was not a convicted felon; (2) he was 18 or older; and (3) he was not in violation of any state law regarding such a purchase. The affidavit would be forwarded by registered mail to the highest-ranking law-enforcement official of the purchaser's place of residence, identifying the firearm to be shipped on return of the receipt. It would also limit the importation of military firearms such as the Italian Mannlicher Carcano rifle bought by Lee Harvey Oswald for $12.78 to assassinate President Kennedy.

WHAT COULD BE simpler or more straightforward or more essential to the enforcement of state laws? And yet many people have been led to believe the bill is some kind of Federal gun registration law. Others have been hoodwinked into thinking that the right of law-abiding citizens to keep a firearm for home protection or for hunting would be forbidden.

Some have been purposely misinformed that the bill controls the purchase of ammunition. Some have been alarmed by statements of gun lobbyists that it places a sales or stamp tax on guns, and that the bill would create some kind of gun monopoly that would put honest dealers, manufacturers or gun servicemen out of business.

There is not the slightest basis for any of these beliefs but it serves well the purposes of those who wish to defeat the bill thus to confuse, obscure, misquote.

The bill, in truth, is a beginning toward preventing guns from coming so easily into the hands of the wrong people. It is a first practical step toward seeing that the almost one million guns sold each year by mail do not go directly into the hands of those who plan to use them for bank robberies, holdups, murders or for sniper killings by the mentally disturbed or hatemongers.

Let me mention two or three cases as examples.

Victor H. Feguer wrote to me while he was waiting to be executed that he wanted to die. He protested vigorously efforts to appeal his case. In the course of an investigation, I found that the records of the Federal Prison Bureau showed that Feguer, within a month of the date he was discharged from the state penitentiary, had bought a .380-caliber automatic revolver over the counter of a Milwaukee gun store. No questions were asked, no identification sought. A casual inquiry probably would have developed the fact that there was something wrong with him because he was paranoid and threatening. A somewhat deeper inquiry would have revealed that he was an ex-convict, had been diagnosed by the prison as a borderline schizophrenic and had a record of crime and juvenile delinquency dating back to his 11th birthday.

Thus armed, Feguer kidnapped a greatly admired and conscientious Iowa doctor and shot and killed him for no reason anyone has been able to learn. That murder could have been prevented under the Dodd bill, because no licensed dealer could have sold Feguer, an ex-prisoner, a revolver.

There are dozens of such cases in Prison Bureau files, including that of a prisoner we reluctantly had to discharge from the Leavenworth penitentiary as the law required. We knew he was extremely dangerous. While en route to Los Angeles, he bought a gun in Flagstaff, Ariz. He had the money, so no questions were asked. When he was later questioned about a check he was trying to cash in a Sears, Roebuck store in California, he whipped out his gun and shot two policemen dead.

ALBERT LEE NUSSBAUM, like Charles J. Whitman, has been a "gun-nut" since he was 18. One exhibit prized by Senator Dodd's committee is a high-powered antitank machine gun that Nussbaum simply bought over the counter.

In 1957 he was sent to prison for five years for transporting a machine gun across the state lines. Within a few months after sentence expired, Nussbaum led eight bank robberies, netting his gang a total of $248,541. During one robbery, of the Lafayette National Bank in Brooklyn, a bank guard was ruthlessly machine-gunned to death and another police officer missed death only because the bullet intended for him lodged in his shield pin. An arsenal belonging to Nussbaum contained 17 revolvers, an automatic carbine rifle, four bullet-proof vests and several thousand rounds of ammunition. When these weapons were traced, it was found most of them had come from so-called "legitimate" sources.

Nussbaum now matter-of-factly says from his cell in a Federal prison, where he is serving a life term, that he is opposed to any firearms controls. He doubts they will work. Perhaps he reached this conclusion from reading the literature of the National Rifle Association — to which he was once admitted without the necessity of disclosing his prison record or much of anything else. Being a member of the N.R.A., he had the incidental advantage of buying a war surplus .45-caliber automatic pistol for $17.50 and an M-l carbine for $20. He also got free ammunition from supplies made available to the N.RA. and affiliated gun clubs by the Government.

Incidentally, these "surplus" carbines, pistols and Springfield '03 rifles are available only to N.R.A. members. They may be "surplus" but they certainly are not museum pieces. In 1965 a total of 848 successful bank holdups involved losses of $3,899,465, according to the American Bankers Association, as bandits armed with handguns, shotguns or rifles more than doubled their attacks and their annual hike between 1961 and 1965. No wonder bank insurance rates increase regularly.

ONE OF THE time-worn arguments against attempting to control the sale of firearms is that it will not stop crime. Opponents of regulation ask: Why try, and in the process perhaps inconvenience law-abiding people?

In this spirit Senator Russell Long of Louisiana, the Assistant Majority Leader, recently said: "These bills might make it more difficult for the murderers to get guns, but the man who intends to kill can always get a gun, no matter what we do."

If the majority of our lawmakers followed such a philosophy there would be no laws against the distribution of narcotics, fraud or check forgery, rape, arson or other crimes. By the unwillingness of some legislators to face up to facts about guns, murder, bank robbery and violence are made easy.

Take Watts, for instance. There, in the most elemental sort of guerrilla warfare, policemen, firemen and innocent bystanders were rifled down from rooftops, moving cars, the ruins of gutted buildings. Fear of snipers' bullets halted efforts to rescue the wounded, stop the looting or douse the fires. Gov. Edmund Brown's tour of the area and his plans to confer with the leaders of the community came to naught because of widespread rifle fire.

During the rioting more than 2,000 guns were seized; one-third were later submitted as evidence of criminal activity. Of those snipers who could be found and arrested, 76 had pistols in their possession and 39 others had shotguns or rifles. Fifty of the 76 persons arrested for having handguns had either a misdemeanor or felony record. Of the 39 arrested with long guns, 28 had previous criminal records. Investigations of the Senate Juvenile Delinquency Committee revealed that all but a few of these guns were acquired prior to the riot and could not, of course, have been legally purchased — had the proposed bill been law. But whatever the figures, it is abundantly clear that there were too many guns in too many violent hands in Watts.

Further, we know that enough weapons have been seized by police elsewhere from Black Muslims to constitute a fearsome warning. South Carolina's Law Enforcement Bureau a few years ago came upon a large cache of rifles, revolvers and ammunition; in the course of questioning a man attempting to buy the guns to carry back to New York, he admitted to being a Black Muslim. There is ample testimony from those who have infiltrated such organizations as the Muslims, the Ku Klux Klan, the Progressive Labor party and the Minutemen that their strategy of violent takeover is dependent on access to lethal weapons. The rise of these groups may account for the short supply of small arms in mailorder houses.

Seaport Traders, of Los Angeles, one of the largest dealers in imported weaponry, is not doing too badly in supplying the demand. Between 1961 and 1963 the company sold 11,427 surplus, rebuilt or rebored foreign revolvers and stub-barreled automatics by mail. The records of the Chicago Police Department indicate that 4,069 went to residents of that city. Twenty-five per cent of the guns, or 948, were delivered to persons having criminal records.

Seaport Traders also undersells most competitors by buying guns in West Germany, dismantling them there and then shipping the serially numbered parts by various means of transportation to several shops in Los Angeles where they are reassembled. The object of all this is the lower tariff rate on parts than on finished guns. The rate on parts is 42 per cent and the rate for each assembled gun is $1.35 plus 30 per cent duty. On the approximately 90,000 guns Seaport Traders has imported, the estimated saving was $49,000. The gun trade has always been a profitable business — whether the guns went to the Indians in frontier days or go to the Radical Right of our day.

IN THOSE SEVEN states which have made an effort to control gun sales (an effort enfeebled by lack of supporting Federal legislation) gun murder rates are considerably lower than in states with few or no regulatory protections. In New York, despite all its problems of social, racial and economic stress, the gun murder rate is less than half the rate in Nebraska, Colorado, Arizona, Montana or Texas, where the principal opposition to Federal firearms legislation originates.

Two Texans at least — President Johnson and Senator Ralph Yarborough — do not go along with their fellow-Texan, Senator John Tower, who said in a recent speech: "I will not support and I hope the

Senate does not see fit to enact legislation which would abridge the right of the people to keep and bear arms."

This familiar argument — that the Second Amendment to the Constitution forbids any attempt to regulate the sale of firearms — is the main standby of the National Rifle Association, particularly Franklin L. Orth, its executive vice president. The brief answer to the argument is this: There is no such amendment to the Constitution as quoted toy Senator Tower. He does not mention the modifying phrase in the amendment's language, namely: "A well-regulated militia being necessary to the security of a free state, the right of the people to keep and bear arms shall not be infringed."

The United States Supreme Court long ago made it clear, in upholding the National Firearms Act, that the amendment did not guarantee to any particular individual the right to bear arms. This right must have, in the words of the Court, "some reasonable relationship to the preservation or efficiency of a well-regulated militia."

Furthermore, Justices of the Supreme Court who were far more conservative than the majority of the present Court have upheld time and time again the right of the Federal Government, in the exercise of its power to regulate commerce, to pass laws restricting the interstate transportation of goods that are in violation of state statutes.

Mr. Orth's effort to use the Second Amendment argument before the House of Delegates of the American Bar Association was resoundingly rejected by an almost unanimous vote. The Bar Association not only found the Dodd bill constitutional but overwhelmingly approved it as sound public policy.

THE MUMBO JUMBO about the right to bear arms is only one part of the smokescreen thrown up by the National Rifle Association to block any gun-control legislation. The association piously declares it favors legislation that would keep firearms out of the hands of criminals, juveniles and incompetents, but has no effective bill of its own. Instead, the N.R.A. protests its concern for proper use of firearms in full-page ads beneath a large photograph of Franklin D. Roosevelt holding a rifle as a young man ("America Needs More Straight Shooters"). In fact, as President, Roosevelt approved the Federal Firearms Act and the National Firearms Act, which control the interstate transportation of machine guns and sawed-off shotguns.

The long-standing efforts of the National Rifle Association to thwart any Federal control of firearms where possible, or to water down bills such as the National Firearms Act, which they could not defeat entirely, is interestingly and exhaustively detailed in Carl Bakal's recent book, "The Right to Bear Arms."

As a substitute for the Dodd the N.R.A. urges one by Congressman Robert Casey of Texas, which the association claims is directed at the criminal and not the gun. Under the Casey proposal the Federal Government would be given jurisdiction over any crime committed by a person armed with a gun that had been transported in interstate commerce.

Thus, 99 per cent of handguns, rifles and shotguns would be covered.

By this legislative legerdemain tens of thousands of local crimes now dealt with under the police powers of the states would become a Federal responsibility. (Incidentally, the original Casey bill prescribed a mandatory minimum penalty of 25 years but this was later reduced to 10 years.)

Apart from the serious constitutional problems involved here, the whole idea is at odds with the universally held principle of local responsibility for crime control. Moreover, the long and dreary history of man's efforts to control crime by torture, banishment, cruel and inhuman punishment shows the futility of long prison terms. For example, armed robbery everywhere now carries severe penalties, and in some states it is punishable by death, yet armed robberies continue to escalate.

The wonder is that the National Rifle Association, an organization of 750,000 sensible men and women, would underwrite, at an annual cost of $2-million, publicity programs based on deceptive reasoning.

Perhaps the answer is: Anything goes that will confuse or obscure the basic issues.

For this reason, perhaps, the N.R.A. argues that the Dodd bill would disarm the citizenry, leaving us helpless pawns of Communists in case of a war in which our missile capability was destroyed, our naval and air power demolished and our armies defeated. Time and again, it has been shown that the Dodd bill in no way restricts the purchase or ownership of a firearm by responsible adults. But fears that the bill would facilitate a Communist takeover nevertheless are soberly advanced in opposition to the bill. Defense Secretary Robert McNamara has testified that "no function of the Department of Defense will be in any way impaired by the enactment of this [Dodd] legislation." And he added his "deep personal conviction about the desirability" of the bill.

PUTTING ASIDE THE sophistry of the gun lobby for the moment, the vital question is: What kind of state law is reasonable and fair?

Only a few advocates of the strictest kind of firearms control believe that the registration and identification of the estimated 100 million pistols, revolvers, rifles, shotguns, pellet guns, bazookas, zip guns and so on is feasible at this time. The development of electronic data processing and information retrieval indicates it may some day become feasible but whether any such Federal law is worth discussing now is doubtful.

That being so, what sort of law regulating the sale of firearms is within reason? Even the National Rifle Association talks about the need to control the indiscriminate sale of handguns. So do most of the western Senators led by Roman L. Hruska of Nebraska. The N.R.A. balks, however, at any attempt to regulate the sale of rifles and shotguns. It does not challenge the figures of the Federal Bureau of Investigation that 30 per cent of willfull killings are committed by persons armed with rifles or shotguns. Yet the N.R.A. argues that a "vast amount of hardship, burden, inconvenience and harshness should not be visited upon those who seek to buy, sell and trade long guns." The "hardships" and "inconvenience," of course, are the unconscionable burden of filling out a form testifying to the fact the seller or buyer is not a drug addict, a convicted felon, a juvenile or a person who has ever been committed to a mental hospital.

After it is agreed, as it must be, that the sale of long guns as well as handguns must be covered by state legislation, the next question is whether we should require a waiting period before the gun is delivered, and if so, for how long? The primary purpose of the delay (it should be at least seven working days) is to allow time for the police to verify the application and to make certain the weapon is not intended for transfer to an irresponsible. A secondary purpose is to permit a cooling-off period for those who may rashly be considering avenging some real or fancied wrong, or destroying themselves or their loved ones in a fit of deep despondency.

In the Washington suburb where I live, a neighbor, Mrs. Doris Crowley, shot herself to death with a gun she had bought just three hours earlier.

Not long afterward, across the river in Virginia, the emotionally disturbed wife of a school principal shot and killed her four children and herself with a pistol she had bought shortly before in a neighborhood store. Such tragedies, in all probability, could be prevented were it impossible to get immediate delivery on a gun.

Once the Dodd bill is passed and state laws become enforceable, local action may make it possible for the police to arrest the ineligible pistol toter before he has an opportunity to commit a crime of violence. Not only should the sale of guns to felons or fugitives or drug addicts be banned but their possession by such persons ought to be subject to punishment. The enactment of such local legislation would mean that everyone who owned a handgun, and possibly also those who owned high-powered rifles, would be required to obtain a certificate of eligibility. Thus, we would be able to seize the guns now in the hands of criminally dangerous persons.

Finally, to implement this most valuable crime deterrent, a state law should be passed restricting the sale of ammunition to those who displayed a certificate of eligibility to own the gun for which ammunition is sought. The legitimate gun owner would have a registration card similar to those issued to automobile owners attesting his rightful ownership of a particular gun and his eligibility to purchase ammunition for it.

THESE ARE SIMPLE, reasonable proposals which would not handicap the honest sportsman or gun enthusiast. They are a small price to pay to reduce the nearly 6,000 fatal shootings that occur each year and the 35,000 assaults made with firearms. As certain as night follows day, they would have some effect on avoidable bloodshed caused by guns that have brought death to more Americans — 750,000 — since the turn of the century than all our wars combined. The annual total of 45,000 armed robberies would also decline instead of increasing, as at present, if no ammunition were available to the illegitimate possessors of handguns. But states that pass laws of this type will enact mere pieces of paper unless they are backed by a Federal statute forbidding circumvention through mail-order sales from states without such legislation.

We are quick enough to blame the courts for a rising crime wave because they insist that the police comply with the Constitution in their treatment of suspects. We have bumper stickers urging "Support Your Police." We appoint crime commissions to philosophize about basic causes of crime. We wring our hands vainly about the shocking killing of 14 innocent Texans and the wounding of more than 30 others by a demented gun nut. We view with alarm the slaughter of five people in Connecticut and the wounding of six others by two gun-slingers. These tragedies happened this year. And on each remaining day of 1966 15 people will be murdered with guns.

This carnage will go on and will increase unless the seven out of ten people who, according to a Gallup poll, believe in firearms control make known their views to their Senators and Congressmen.

Gun Curb Fight Opens in Capital

BY BEN A. FRANKLIN | APRIL 9, 1967

WASHINGTON, APRIL 8 — The growing and often bitter campaign for and against the passage of Federal firearms controls reached an unusual, double-feature climax here this week.

On the same day that a House Judiciary subcommittee opened hearings on President Johnson's request for strict firearms control, the National Rifle Association convened its 96th annual meeting, devoting a major part of the week's agenda to organizing opposition to all legislation in Congress, particularly the Administration bill.

The meeting was given a sharply worded prediction by Senator Edward M. Kennedy that some form of gun control proposals, which have failed to clear Congress every year since the assassination of President Kennedy, would finally pass, despite the N.R.A.'s mobilization of its 800,000 members against it.

An estimated total of 10,000 members of the Rifle Association were here this week. But because of the association's policy of discussing legislation only beyond closed doors, Senator Kennedy was asked to deliver an address that he had hoped to make last Sunday before the membership to a closed meeting of the 75-man board of directors.

According to officials of a group that was organized recently to oppose the N.R.A. campaign — the first such national antigun organization in the country — the effort to sway public opinion on gun control is an unequal contest.

The N.R.A. annual operating report for 1966, distributed at this week's convention, disclosed the following about the association's $5.1 million tax-exempt income in that year:

The N.R.A. legislative and public affairs division spent $453,683 in 1966, an increase of nearly $40,000 over 1963. The total did not include $113,000 listed for the first time in 1966 for "public relations campaign" costs.

The association circulated a record 9.8-million copies of The American Rifleman, a monthly magazine that contains statements of its positions against gun legislation and criticism of efforts to curb gun sales.

Some 28 per cent, or $1,356,054 of 1966 income, had come from firearms and sporting goods manufacturers' advertisements in The American Rifleman.

AIDS N.R.A. POLICY

The N.R.A. distributed 108,100 news releases in 1966, besides a wide range of gun safety material sent to newspapers, magazines and radio and television stations.

Association officials also confirmed that they signed a contract last May with a New York public relations firm, the Infoplan Division of Communications Affiliates, Inc., a subsidiary of the Interpublic Group of Companies, Inc. Neither N.R.A. spokesmen nor Richard Wilcox, Infoplan's N.R.A. account executive, would disclose the cost of the public relations contract.

Mr. Wilcox said in a telephone interview from New York that the agency "counsels the N.R.A. on policy and helps prepare communications campaigns at every level, directed to many audiences, including women and children. We have absolutely nothing to do with legislation."

"How much they pay us is their business and ours, I would think," Mr. Wilcox said. Asked if the fee was "about $1-million," William Gilmour, an N.R.A. staff publicist here, commented, "They don't do anything cheap, but it's not more than $1-million."

Members of the newly organized National Council for a Responsible Firearms Policy said that after three months of seeking operations funds from private sources, its founders have "given up trying to get any foundation money."

The Rev. J. Elliott Corbett, secretary of the council, said its officers were "paying out their own money for postage."

"We are attempting to build lists of people who will help us, state by state," Mr. Corbett said. "We think Congressmen respond to their own people." Mr. Corbett is director of the Washington Study Program of the Methodist Church.

Members of the council, including Mayor Lindsay and James V. Bennett, retired director of the Federal Bureau of Prisons — both officers of the new organization — testified this week before Representative Emanuel Celler's subcommittee in support of the Administration gun bill.

While they were testifying, however, hundreds of N.R.A. members visited their Congressmen, armed with opposition data distributed at the N.R.A. convention.

To counter the impression the N.R.A. opposes all gun legislation, staff spokesmen said, its newly elected president, Harold W. Glassen of Lansing, Mich., said at a news conference here Thursday that the association would submit to Congress its own "new proposals."

They are to include proposed restrictions on the mail-order sale of pistols and a "Federal commission" to screen and thus reduce the importation of cheap foreign military surplus weapons — guns Mr. Glassen described as "junk," unsuitable for sporting or target use.

The N.R.A. spokesmen acknowledged that the mail-order proposal suggested by Mr. Glassen was a retreat from the association's 1964 position, when it strongly favored a bill in the Senate that would have applied to mail-order sales of pistols, rifles and shotguns.

Gun Curbs Backed by a Rifle Expert

BY DOUGLAS ROBINSON | AUG. 26, 1967

A BRONX MEMBER of Congress who has won four national championship medals from the National Rifle Association offered support yesterday for city legislation to control the sale of rifles and shotguns.

Democratic Representative James H. Scheuer told a City Council hearing that he owned two shotguns, three rifles and a .32-caliber revolver. He said he had a permit for the revolver, as required by state law.

"It's insanity to believe that my civil rights are being violated by having to have a pistol permit," he declared. He added that he would have no objection to a law requiring him to obtain a similar permit for his other weapons.

"No responsible citizen can in good conscience deny the urgent need to protect the public from arming the destructive, deranged, dangerous and irresponsible persons among us," he told the hearing.

TWO-DAY HEARING ENDS

The National Rifle Association has consistently lobbied against any type of Federal, State or local control over the sale of rifles and shotguns.

Mr. Scheuer's testimony was given on the second and last day of hearings conducted by the Council's Subcommittee on Firearms Control and the State Joint Legislative Committee on Firearms Control at City Hall.

The Council is considering local laws that would require the registration and licensing of city residents who purchase or own any type of firearms. State law now demands that permits be obtained only for guns that can be concealed on the person.

Present laws also forbid a convicted felon to possess a rifle, define machine guns as contraband, prohibit the carrying of a rifle not in a sheath on the city streets, and bar the fifing of a rifle or shotgun within city limits.

The Councilmen are also studying a resolution urging the Legislature to require permits or all firearms.

Yesterday's hearing in the Council chamber was dramatically interrupted shortly before 1 P.M. by Councilman Theodore Weiss, Democrat-Liberal of Manhattan, who broke into the testimony of a witness to say:

"I just want to say that George Lincoln Rockwell, a man whose political philosophy I abhor, has been assassinated, apparently by rifle fire."

The announcement caused no noticeable stir in the audience of some 50 persons, many of whom represented gun clubs opposed to the legislation.

TIMELINESS IS SEEN

Later, Mr. Weiss told newsmen that the murder of Mr. Rockwell in Arlington, Va., "demonstrates again the timeliness of these hearings."

"The violence that is rampant has no political discrimination — it hits the left and the right, the young and the old," he said. "This senseless carnage must be controlled. I don't know how much longer we will go on allowing people to be killed senselessly."

Councilman Joseph Modugno, Republican-Conservative of Queens, who has indicated his opposition to the proposed laws, took issue with Mr. Weiss, saying that "it was highly improper of him to announce Rockwell's death at the hearings."

"It is not at all relevant," he said. "We already know we have a serious crime problem,but no local gun registration, such as we are considering here, would help in the least — it would only lull people into a false sense of security."

The gun control hearing was disrupted briefly in the late morning when Herman B. Glaser, chairman of the New York Council for City Affairs, walked into the Council chamber carrying a large floral box wrapped in white paper and tied with a pink ribbon. He was accompanied by a blaze of television lights.

Mr. Weiss, noticing the commotion, asked Mr. Glaser if there were a rifle in the box. Receiving an affirmative answer, he ordered Mr. Glaser and his gaily wrapped package out of the chamber.

A RIFLE AND ROSES

Outside, Mr. Glaser, who heads a nonprofit group composed of bankers, legislators and others interested in civic problems, opened the box for newsmen. Inside were a .22-caliber target gun and six long-stemmed red roses.

Later, during his testimony in support of the legislation, Mr. Glaser said he had merely been trying to show that anyone carrying a lethal weapon could walk by policemen and marshals. Newsmen had been notified that he would take the package to the hearing.

Among those who spoke in favor of the gun bills was John P. Lomenzo, New York Secretary of State, who called for a "drastic overhaul of archaic and ineffective city and state laws to effect greater firearms control over all weapons, including rifles and shotguns."

Other advocates of tighter laws included Representative Jonathan B. Bingham, Democrat of the Bronx; State Senator Manfred Ohrenstein, Democrat-Liberal of Manhattan; District Attorney Aaron E. Koota of Brooklyn; and Vincent J. Dermody, Assistant District Attorney in charge of the Manhattan homicide bureau. Opponents of the measures were led by Mrs. Maria Monplaisir, a member of the state executive committee of the Conservative party. She told the hearing that statistics showed the legislation "will not cure crime by one iota."

"These proposed laws will not reduce crime because they are not really aimed at the criminal who uses a gun in committing a crime, but at the sportsman or hunter who uses a gun for hunting and harmless target shooting," she said.

Mark K. Benenson, a lawyer and spokesman for the New York Sporting Arms Association, Inc., said gun laws had "demonstrated no measurable value in reducing crime."

He said his group opposed the proposed bill that would require a notice of intention to purchase rifles and shotguns, as well as another requiring registration. He did endorse a bill that would compel gun dealers to notify the police of all firearms sales within 24 hours.

Opposition was also voiced by representatives of gun clubs, firearms collectors and hunters.

A Gun Is Power, Black Panther Says

BY WALLACE TURNER | **MAY 21, 1967**

SAN FRANCISCO, MAY 20 — Huey Newton toyed with a foot-long stiletto that he said he had taken from an American Nazi party officer in a scuffle last weekend.

Across the room, a bodyguard named Sherwin held a 12-gauge shotgun between his knees. In an easy chair, Warren, another guard, shifted the 45-caliber automatic in its holster. On the sofa, Terry, a karate expert, flexed his muscles.

The sun was hot through the windows, and down below at the Haight-Asbury intersection, the hippies chatted and laughed and avowed that life was made for us to love one another.

"Political power comes through the barrel of a gun," Mr. Newton said.

The 25-year-old Negro sees himself as the organizer of a new force in American politics. It is called the Black Panther Party for Self Defense. Its members electrified the California Legislative Assembly three weeks ago by crowding into the chamber, carrying shotguns rifles and pistols.

MOVED BY BOMB THREAT

The Black Panther group (named for the political group organized among Negroes in Alabama) has headquarters on a busy street in Oakland, but the interview could not be held there.

"I was told someone was going to bomb our headquarters," said Mr. Newton, the Panther's minister of defense. So he adjourned the appointment to a friend's home in San Francisco.

What the slender young man talks in his rapid, well modulated voice is black nationalism. He admires Malcolm X, the late black nationalist leader; W. E. B. DuBois, a founder of the National Association for the Advancement of Colored People who later became a Communist;

Stokley Carmichael, a leading "black power" advocate, and Nat (the prophet) Turner, who led a slave revolt in 1822.

Mr. Newton came to Oakland with his parents in 1945 and went through Oakland public schools and the two-year-city college. He went to law school here for a year, and intends to go back next fall.

He does not list the Rev. Dr. Martin Luther King Jr. as one of his admired Negro leaders, explaining:

"We do not believe in passive and nonviolent tactics. They haven't worked for us black people. They are bankrupt."

The Black Panther symbol suits his organization's aims, Mr. Newton explained, because the black panther will not attack anyone, but will back up, but when he's cornered will strike out and will not stop until the aggressor is wiped out thoroughly, wholly, absolutely and completely.

"We are here to defend ourselves and our black communities," Mr. Newton said.

Asked how many members he had, Mr. Newton quoted Malcolm X in an answer to a different question: "Those who know don't say and those who say don't know."

The members have ranks, and the name of the ranks (which he would not give) designate the service the member is called on to give. His bodyguards, Terry, Warren, and Sherwin, had the ranks of captain.

At the Black Panther meetings the discussion centers on "racist imperialist America."

Asked about the war, Mr. Newton said:

"I believe the racist American army should withdraw from Vietnam. The situation in Vietnam is similar to here. It's a police action going on in Vietnam. The army is not there to protect them, but to brutalize and murder their women and children."

He said the Black Panthers would refuse to report for draft induction.

Asked about conditions at home, Mr. Newton said:

"The situation here in America is that the police are in our communities not to protect us. They are here to contain us, to oppress us, to brutalize us."

When armed members of his organization entered the legislative chamber, they said that they were protesting proposed gun-control legislation. Mr. Newton explained:

"We wanted them to know we will continue to arm black people in spite of any legislation that is passed. We weren't trying to influence what they did. Our message was to point out that the plot to disarm black America would fail."

The Black Panthers buy their guns openly at gun stores, he said, although there is trouble sometimes. Mr. Newton said that "many racists control the gun stores" and the Panthers are turned down when they try to buy.

Organization members carry their guns openly, the side-arms at their hips, and the shotguns or rifles on their shoulders or held with both hands across their chests. This is legal under California law, which only forbids carrying concealed weapons without a permit.

Some laws in the fish and game code cover firing guns from moving vehicles, but these do not inhibit the weapon displays by the Black Panthers.

When they disrupted the legislative assembly, authorizes found difficulty in placing a charge. Eventually the charge of conspiracy to disrupt the Legislature was placed. It is pending.

Mr. Newton gave this view of the Black Panther purpose:

"If any person in the black community was being brutalized or murder was being attempted by the occupying army [the police] it would be my duty to come to the person's defense." If it meant killing the aggressor, this is the tactic the Black Panther would use.

"Force, guns and arms are the real political arena," he said. "Decisions against the black people are always backed up by racist police forces and racist military force."

Dodd Gun-Control Law Opposed by Big Rifle Group at a Hearing

BY BEN A. FRANKLIN | JULY 20, 1967

WASHINGTON, JULY 19 — Officials of the National Rifle Association and other sportsmen's organizations testified today that the Johnson Administration's proposed Federal gun control law would unfairly restrict the legitimate ownership of firearms by law-abiding citizens and have virtually no effect on crime.

In their testimony, the officials of the N.R.A. — the biggest national firearms organization, with more than 800,000 members — said there was no evidence of "causal relationships" between the easy availability of guns and crime or rioting.

They testified on conflicting gun control measures, one sponsored for the Administration by Senator Thomas J. Dodd, Democrat of Connecticut, and the other for sportsmen's groups by Senator Roman L. Hruska, Republican of Nebraska.

The organization is supporting Mr. Hruska's bill to regulate the interstate, mail-order sale of pistols.

'FAIR PLAY' CITED

But its spokesmen told the Senate Juvenile Delinquency subcommittee today that Mr. Dodd's proposal to prohibit all interstate commerce in mail-order handguns and, further, to regulate the sale of long guns — shotguns and rifles — would be discriminatory, unduly restrictive on rural Americans and "contrary to the American spirit of balance and fair play."

Today was the first day of testimony against gun control, and it disclosed again the ideological chasm between members of Congress with urban constituencies, worried about crime and violence, and those from thinly-populated rural states, particularly in the West, where a gun is regarded as "a necessity."

JOHN OLSON/THE LIFE IMAGES COLLECTION/GETTY IMAGES

Senator Thomas J. Dodd was an outspoken advocate for stricter gun laws.

As Senator Frank Church, Democrat of Idaho, put it in strongly opposing any Federal firearms legislation, "Guns come close to the feeling of sovereignty itself among our people. This is an issue that cuts right to the bone.

In Idaho, he said, it is "entirely impractical to rely solely on law enforcement agencies in remote rural areas."

"Help may be an hour away," he said.

Referring to his own Nebraska constituency, Senator Hruska, a subcommittee member, said that "to deter criminals in the country-side is a little bit different than in New York City, where [because of New York's strong gun registration law] only 17,000 of more than 8 million people have permits to own guns."

"The intruder breaking into an apartment in New York has it made because he knows there is no one to shoot back," he said. He insisted that Mr. Dodd and Senator Edward M. Kennedy, Democrat of Massachusetts, the two aggressive supporters of the Administration bill on

EARLY GUN CONTROL MEASURES **43**

the subcommittee, had "shown no proof, only assertions," that restrictive gun laws deterred crime.

Harold W. Glassen, a Michigan lawyer and sportsman, who is the elected president of the rifle association, told the committee that "it would be just as logical for us to legislate automobiles, airplanes and any other sharp, blunt, corrosive or poisonous substance that could possibly be used in aid in the commission of a crime or to accomplish self-destruction."

The philosophy behind Mr. Dodd's bill, Mr. Glassen said, "is that guns shall not be available except to certain specified persons."

"Sportsmen disapprove of that type of legislation," he said. "They feel that the philosophy behind any measure to regulate firearms should be that firearms be available except to certain types of persons, such as felons and juveniles."

Gun Control Added to Civil Rights Bill by Senate, 72 to 23

BY MARJORIE HUNTER | MARCH 7, 1968

WASHINGTON, MARCH 6 — The Senate added limited gun control provisions today to the civil rights bill.

The amendment, designed to stem the flow of firearms and other weapons to would-be rioters, was offered by a Southern conservative, Senator Russell B. Long, Democrat of Louisiana.

His proposal was quickly embraced by liberals who have been trying for years to get effective gun control legislation through Congress.

The amendment, accepted by a vote of 72 to 23, would make it a Federal crime to teach or demonstrate the use or making of firearms, fire-bombs or other explosive devices meant for use in a riot or other civil disorder.

This falls short of proposals pending in Congress for several years that would impose strict Federal control on the interstate sale and purchase of firearms.

However, backers of the stiffer gun control bills viewed the Senate action today as a foot in the door. Among those backing the Long amendment were Edward M. Kennedy, Democrat of Massachusetts; Robert F. Kennedy, Democrat of New York, and Thomas J Dodd, Democrat of Connecticut, the chief sponsor of strong gun control legislation.

Rioting and other civil disorders, rather than civil rights, continued to dominate the Senate debate today.

Until yesterday, debate had centered on the twin features of the compromise civil rights bill — open housing and Federal protection of Negroes and civil rights workers.

The bill was expanded yesterday to make it a Federal crime to cross state lines with intent to incite a riot. A riot was defined as a public disturbance involving violence during an assemblage of three or more persons.

Asserting that the approved antiriot amendment was virtually worthless, Senator Long sought today to crack down still harder on those inciting riots.

His first proposal, narrowly defeated, 48 to 47, would have made it a Federal crime to incite a riot, whether or not the inciter had crossed state lines.

"This is what is needed if you want to do something about Stokely Carmichael and Rap Brown," Senator Long said, referring to two militant Negro leaders.

His proposal, Senator Long argued, would have been applicable in major riots in the Watts area of Los Angeles, Detroit, Newark and elsewhere.

The Senate also rejected, 64 to 27, another Long proposal that would have made it a Federal offense to commit or threaten "any unlawful act of violence" in support of a civil disorder. This would include "sniping and shooting at persons with any firearm.

This proposal found the Kennedy brothers arguing on opposite sides.

Edward Kennedy suggested that the proposal would grant far too much power to the Federal Government in general and the Federal Bureau of Investigation in particular.

Robert Kennedy said he would welcome such as expansion of Federal power. Noting that he had no such powers during his three years as Attorney General, Senator Kennedy added, with a half smile:

"Why, this could change the whole complexion of the civil rights struggle. If three persons were shot in Selma, Ala., the Federal Government could move right in. I congratulate the gentleman from Louisiana."

The Senate later agreed, by voice vote, to make it a Federal crime to interfere with policemen and firemen carrying out their duties during a riot. This, too, was proposed by Senator Long.

But it rejected, also by voice vote, another Long proposal that would have made it a Federal crime to loot during a civil disorder. Opponents argued that action against looting could be handled by the local police.

Gun Control Bill Speeded by House

BY JOHN W. FINNEY | JUNE 6, 1968

WASHINGTON, JUNE 5 — The House, spurred by the shooting of Senator Robert F. Kennedy, moved quickly today toward adoption of broad anticrime legislation, including controls over interstate sales of handguns.

By a 317-to-60 vote, the House rejected a move to send the crime control legislation, passed last month by the Senate, to a Senate-House conference. The vote cleared the way for the House to accept the Senate version tomorrow and send the legislation to the White House.

In lonely opposition, Representative Emanuel Cellar, Brooklyn Democrat, who is chairman of the House Judiciary Committee, vainly protested before a hushed but emotional House that the Senate bill was a "cruel hoax" and "bursting at the seams with unconstitutional provisions."

But in the hour-long debate it became evident that for the majority of the House the Kennedy shooting was but the final confirmation that legislative steps should be taken to curb violence.

'NO FURTHER QUIBBLING'

"Surely there can be no further quibbling about the urgent need for tougher law enforcement legislation," the House Republican leader, Gerald R. Ford of Michigan, observed at one point in a statement that seemed to reflect the mood of the House.

The House last year passed the Administration's crime control bill providing for Federal grants to states and local communities to improve and strengthen law enforcement agencies. But to the House bill the Senate added three controversial provisions not considered by the House and opposed to some degree by the Administration.

One of the Senate provisions would overturn recent Supreme Court decisions establishing the constitutional rights of criminal suspects. A second would authorize court-supervised wiretapping and electronic eavesdropping against a broad variety of crimes. The third would restrict interstate sales of handguns.

A staff member of the Senate Juvenile Delinquency subcommittee said the .22-caliber Iver Johnson revolver, identified by the Los Angeles police as the one used in the shooting, was a "pot metal" weapon particularly made for the cut-rate mail order trade.

The gun is made by Iver Johnson's Arms and Cycle Works, Inc. of Fitchburg, Mass., a wholesale gun manufacturer. The weapon, according to the subcommittee aide, costs $15 to $18 when sold retail through the mail.

Senator Kennedy had supported the Senate gun control provision, although, like the Administration, he had contended it should go further and include rifles and shotguns. In his position, he ran into heckling opposition in his campaigning through the Pacific Northwest, the center of much of the opposition to gun control legislation.

Strict Gun Control Practiced Abroad

BY ALBIN KREBS | JUNE 13, 1968

PROPONENTS OF STRICTER gun-control legislation nave asserted that of all the civilized nations of the world, only the United States gives its citizens the "right to bear arms."

In Britain, France, Spain, Belgium, the Soviet Union, Italy, West Germany, Switzerland and many Asian countries, the ownership of firearms is considered a privilege rather than a right, and the privilege is subject to strict legislation.

This fact was noted by President Johnson last week when, in the aftermath of the assassination of Senator Robert F. Kennedy, he called again for strict controls on private ownership of guns.

"Each year in this country, guns are involved in more than 6,500 murders," he said. "This compares with 30 in England, 99 in Canada, 68 in West Germany and 37 in Japan." In addition, guns in private hands, estimated to number 50 million to 200 million, were responsible for 10,000 suicides and 2,600 accidental deaths last year.

BRITAIN IS STRICT

The President noted bitterly that in the United States, firearms — handguns, rifles and shotguns — are as easy to obtain as "baskets of fruit or cartons of cigarettes." A survey by The New York Times disclosed that this is anything but the case elsewhere.

Nobody in Britain may have a firearm by right, according to a spokesman for the Home Office, and anyone who wants one even for hunting must go through a complicated procedure of applying for a certificate before he may even purchase one.

Britain's Firearms Act of 1937 requires that a person who wants to buy a gun must obtain a certificate from the police chief in the area in which he lives. The police chief "must satisfy himself that applicant is not by reason of a criminal record prohibited from possessing a firearm and is not in any other way likely to endanger the public safety or peace."

DEALERS MUST REPORT

A dealer, after seeing the applicant's certificate, must register all transactions involving guns and ammunition, giving the serial number of the weapon, and pass on the information to the local police station. Failure to do so subjects the gun dealer to six months imprisonment.

The purchase of guns by mail order, which would be severely curtailed in proposed legislation in the United States, is permitted in Britain, but with the same restrictions that apply to personal purchases. It is illegal to pawn firearms in Britain. In this country, most states allow the pawning of weapons with little or no controls.

Proposed gun control laws considered by Congress in the last three years would adopt some of the British provisions, such as a requirement that guns sold be registered with the Treasury Department. Opponents of the legislation, led by the National Rifle Association, an organization of gun-fanciers and sportsmen, have maintained that this would result in troublesome red tape.

French gun laws are strict and unambiguous. They stipulate that arms purchasers must be over 21. Mail order sales are banned and all gun sales must be registered. To obtain a permit to buy a gun, the applicant must undergo a background investigation that is long and thorough. It can take as long as six weeks.

In France only the police and licensed guards are permitted to carry loaded firearms. Private persons with properly registered revolvers cannot carry them on their persons under any circumstances.

A Frenchman on his way to a firing range or a pheasant hunt, if he is carrying a gun, cannot even stop for a glass of wine along the way. He must go direct, and his gun must be carried in a box or carrying case, in the trunk and not the glove compartment of his car. Both the clip and firing bolt of the gun must be removed.

Gun-control laws in Italy are similar to those in France. As in France, the applicant must be at least 21 years old, and a certificate of police clearance and registration of the weapon are required.

In Spain, the procedures make it even more difficult to buy a gun. An applicant must tell the director general of security why he wants one, and the director general may deny the request without giving a reason.

50 CARTRIDGES AT A TIME

After the Spaniard gets a purchase permit and buys his gun, he must register it with the nearest post of the Civil Guard, the gendarmerie of Spain, which issues him a "guia," or guide, which must be carried with the license when the weapon is used. Only 50 cartridges for the weapon may be bought at one time, and all purchases of ammunition are entered in the guia.

Crimes in which shooting is involved are said to be rare in Spain.

The Soviet Union's crime rate is unrelated to gun ownership. Private ownership of rifles and revolvers is punishable by as much as two years imprisonment, and press reports indicate that knives are the weapons most often used in homicides.

In most of the Soviet Union, hunters may buy shotguns, but in the far north and Siberia, rifles may be bought with a special permit. They must be registered with the police.

In West Germany, there has been only one case of attempted political murder since World War II. That was the attempt on the life of Rudi Dutschke, the extremist student leader, eight weeks ago.

"Well-reputed and trustworthy citizens" may buy handguns in West Germany, but only if they cite plausible reasons such as a "dangerous" profession or isolated, "dangerous" living quarters, according to the German Firearms Law of 1938.

For pistols, the law also demands a purchase permit and another permit just to carry the weapons outside one's own premises. Rifles may be bought by permit, with the stipulation that the permit be renewed every three years. Purchase permits are retained by the gun dealer, whose records are regularly inspected by the police.

ONE WEAPON EXEMPT

Belgium's laws are strict, but several murders have been carried out with a .22 caliber rifle that is made in Belgium by Fabrique Nationale d'Armes de Guerre. The weapon is exempted from the otherwise tough restrictions on firearms possession, and this is generally attributed to the influence of the manufacturer, the huge Société Générale group of enterprises, a holding company that controls about a third of Belgian industrial activity.

For all pistols and rifles other than the .22, a buyer must obtain a permit signed by the Belgian equivalent of a district attorney, after local police have conducted a thorough investigation of the applicant, which takes one or two months. No weapons are sold through mail order houses.

In Belgium, which has a population of 9.3 million, there were only 71 murders in 1965. The figure also includes murders committed with weapons other than firearms.

In Switzerland murder is not a significant problem even though about 500,000 Swiss in a total population of six million have rifles. Many own the latest model of automatic weapon, kept in perfect working order in a closet at home, along with 24 rounds of ammunition.

LONG TRADITION IN SWITZERLAND

Switzerland's long tradition of arms in the home, consecrated by military law, directs that members of its citizen militia keep their uniforms, rifles, and field packs at home so that they may spring to the defense of their country. All able-bodied males between 20 and 50 have this obligation.

But a spokesman for the Swiss Defense Department said that although no statistics are kept, the misuse of army rifles in citizens' care is rare. Revolvers, pistols and other handguns may be purchased only with a permit.

In the Far East most nations have followed the example of Japan in drafting unusually strict gun-control laws. In Japan, where no one except police officers is permitted to own a revolver, there were only 37 firearms murders last year. In the United States, almost twice Japan's population, there were 6,500 firearms homicides last year.

The Gun Lobby Is Feeling No Pain

BY ROBERT SHERRILL | APRIL 11, 1971

WASHINGTON — There were a few complaints, to be sure, at the centennial convention of the million-member National Rifle Association. Some hunting marshes were said to be laden with spent lead shot (30,000 pellets per acre is not uncommon), and ducks that eat the shot may be a source of lead poisoning for hunters who eat the ducks. But nobody knew what to do about it. So much for ecology. And then there was the warning from one high N.R.A. official that if the District of Columbia government becomes too obnoxious in demanding the employment of minority groups, the N.R.A. just might have to move its headquarters to some more friendly clime — like Virginia, or Indiana. So much for race relations.

But when it came to the basic of all basic goals — freedom from restrictive gun laws — officials of the N.R.A., this town's most powerful lobby, could hardly contain their optimism last week. "Everyone here is thoroughly enjoying himself," said N.R.A. President Woodson D. Scott, and a considerable portion of the enjoyment "stems from the present legislative atmosphere in relation to gun controls."

The N.R.A. had been assured by "important members of the Administration," he said, that there would be no increased effort to curb the traffic in guns, despite the fact that three Presidential commissions in the past four years have urged everything from outlawing the manufacture of handguns to the licensing of all gun owners. And Congress, he said, seemed to be "more sensible" about such matters — perhaps because, as was often mentioned at the convention, politicians had learned a fearsome lesson from the defeat of Senator Joseph Tydings last year. Senator Tydings had been one of the most outspoken advocates of tighter gun controls, and N.R.A. members, who put bumper stickers and heavy money into the campaign against his re-election, claim they made the difference.

Jack Basil, the N.R.A's chief watchdog of Congressional legislation, told the centennial celebrants that he was delighted to be able to report that, of the dozens of restrictive bills introduced in Congress last year, not one had been passed.

With an interpretation that some constitutional scholars approve, and some denounce, the N.R.A. takes its stand on the second half of this statement in the Bill of Rights: "A well regulated militia, being necessary to the security of a free state, the right of the people to keep and bear arms shall not be infringed."

There was a time when Congress, made uncomfortable by the assassinations of John Kennedy, Robert Kennedy, Martin Luther King Jr., seemed almost in the mood to disagree significantly with the N.R.A.; that was before so many of the control movement leaders either dropped out or were defeated, and before their followers became discouraged from such a long struggle that produced so little. But before its deflation of spirit, Congress did pass a few minor reform acts, the most important one being the Gun Control Act of 1968. It outlaws the importation of foreign military surplus guns — leaving more of the "Saturday night special" market to domestic junk gun manufacturers — and sharply restricts the interstate and mail-order sale of rifles and shotguns. (Last week the Supreme Court upheld the law's constitutionality.)

That was the N.R.A.'s darkest hour. Its most dedicated members see it as their Pearl Harbor — a sneak attack by gun control advocates, taking advantage of what N.R.A. banquet speaker Senator Barry Goldwater described as "the present era of hysteria and criticism relative to civilian possession of firearms."

Only by an intensive campaign to educate Congress "beginning now," said Mr. Scott, could the N.R.A, make sure that it would "never again have a situation such as existed in 1968 and prior thereto" — a national and Congressional mood for gun control reform.

There is good reason for the N.R.A.'s cocky aggressiveness. It has paid off before. Within a year after passage of the gun control act, it began coming apart. Originally the purchasers of all ammunition had to register, but in 1969, Congress decided this was too much of a burden on gun merchants, so rifle (except .22 caliber) and shotgun ammunition was exempted from the law. The big drive this year will be to exempt .22-caliber ammunition, too. The House overwhelmingly approved the exemption last year, but a threatened filibuster by Senator Tydings kept it from coming up in the Senate. The N.R.A is also pushing half a dozen bills that would repeal the 1968 act entirely.

Gun control advocates still have a number of statistics to offer, of course: There are an estimated 24 million handguns loose in the land — every year the number jumps by more than two million and the F.B.I. says these are the preferred weapon in one-half of all murders, and in two-thirds of all robberies (up 20 per cent last year).

And along with Senator Edward Kennedy, who at this point appears to be the leader of the pro-control forces (he asked the N.R.A. to let him speak to the convention on his bill to register firearms and license owners, but he was turned down), there are some bright new faces on that side. Among them are Representative Abner Mikva of Illinois, who wants to ban the manufacture and sale of all handguns (he knows what to expect from his colleagues on that one, having run it through, with lumps, when he was in the Illinois State Legislature) and Senator Adlai Stevenson III.

Mr. Stevenson's father killed a cousin in a childhood gun accident. But that isn't why the Senator wants to cut down on the gun traffic. "I just know, from my experience on the Chicago Crime Commission," he said last week, "that there is a connection between crime and the accessibility of guns." He is obviously a first-termer.

CHAPTER 2

The Reagan Years and Shifts in Gun Laws

President Ronald Reagan survived an assassination attempt on March 30, 1981, just two months after he took office. He was struck in the lung by a single bullet and suffered internal bleeding. Although no one died in the attack, White House Press Secretary James Brady was permanently disabled and became a tireless advocate for gun control laws. But the attack on the president did not lead to substantial gun control legislation during his two-term administration, just as gun control advocates had feared when he was first elected.

Gun-Control Advocates Are Feeling Surrounded

BY PHIL GAILEY | DEC. 27, 1981

ONE OF THE darkest hours for handgun control advocates was the election of Ronald Reagan. Suddenly, with Mr. Reagan's inauguration, the battle shifted from winning passage of stiffer handgun control legislation to trying to keep the conservative tide in Congress from sweeping away laws already on the books.

Gun control, like abortion and busing, is one of those emotional issues that Senate Republican leaders managed to keep off the legislative agenda in 1981. The New Right and its Congressional allies did not press these issues during Mr. Reagan's first year, lest they divert attention from the President's economic program.

But in 1982 they will be demanding action on their priorities — including gun control. For his part, Mr. Reagan, a friend and member of the National Rifle Association, has remained steadfast in his opposition to handgun control legislation despite the unsuccessful assassination attempt in March. He announced plans to abolish the Bureau of Alcohol, Tobacco and Firearms, the enforcer of Federal firearms laws, and endorsed a proposal to weaken the 1968 Gun Control Act.

Still, the gloom pervading the handgun control movement seemed to lift recently, when the Senate Judiciary Committee held hearings on the McClure-Volkmer bill to repeal key provisions of the 1968 law — the nation's major legislative attempt to control guns, passed after the assassinations of the Rev. Martin Luther King Jr. and Senator Robert F. Kennedy. They lifted because the hearings proved to be a re-run of an old show.

Senator Charles E. Grassley, Republican of Iowa, who received $65,000 in campaign contributions from pro-gun lobbies in 1980, was the only Senator to show up for the opening session. By midday, after he had excused himself, a committee staff member had to take up the gavel because no Senator was present when Neal Knox, an official of the National Rifle Association, testified.

The absence of senators at the session was perhaps more understandable than significant. The cast had few new faces, the plot had not thickened and the testimony from handpicked witnesses added little to the debate. In short, the hearing had no bang.

There was Richard Boulin, a former policeman from Monrovia, Md., telling how his 1977 conviction for illegally selling firearms from his private collection had made his life miserable. There were Pat and Billie Hayes, who own a gun shop in Basque Farms, N. M., rehashing their 1977 experience with the Bureau of Alcohol, Tobacco and Firearms. Such witnesses have been regulars in Congressional hearings on the gun control issue. In the past they were presented as law-abiding citizens who had suffered harassment at the hands of Federal agents. With the Reagan Administration's announced intention to dismember the bureau and transfer its functions to the Secret Service and the United States Customs service, they were brought back to play a new role in supporting the National Rifle Association and other lobbies in their assault on the 1968 law.

The act, which handgun control advocates contend lacks the teeth to justify its name, was a compromise bill that even the National Rifle Association backed at the time. It requires the licensing of gun dealers and proof of identification by purchasers. It also makes it easier to trace guns used in violent crimes and restricts the sale of guns to convicted felons and those with mental disorders.

According to handgun control organizations that oppose the bill, the proposed Firearm Owner Protection Act, drafted by Senator James A. McClure, Republican of Idaho, and Representative Harold L. Volkmer, Democrat of Missouri, would undo major provisions of the 1968 law.

Among other things, it would limit Federal control of gun dealers, eliminate restrictions on the interstate sale of firearms, force the Government to pay attorney fees in firearms cases it loses, require that the authorities prove that violators intended to break the law and make it easier for convicted felons to purchase guns.

With 57 cosponsors in the Senate and 166 in the House, it might appear that the McClure-Volkmer measure's time has come. Donald E. Fraher, legislative director of Handgun Control Inc., is not so sure.

SUPPORT MAY BE SKIN DEEP

"I think support for the McClure-Volkmer bill is a mile wide and a half inch deep," he said. "It has fewer cosponsors than it did last year. I think a lot of Senators and Congressmen signed on for political reasons, not knowing what the bill would really do. How can any member of Congress be in favor of making it easier for convicted felons to buy a gun when they get out of prison?"

The Reagan Administration has endorsed the McClure-Volkmer position, even though President Reagan's Task Force on Violent Crime recommended the adoption of measures to control the purchase of handguns, including a waiting period and a ban on the importation of parts for the so-called Saturday Night Specials.

In the weeks ahead, handgun control groups will try to change the political climate, shifting the focus back to strengthening, rather than weakening, the 1968 law. The House and Senate Judiciary sub-committees are planning to hold hearings on a Handgun Crime Control Bill sponsored by Senator Edward M. Kennedy, Democrat of Massachusetts, and Representative Peter W. Rodino Jr., Democrat of New Jersey. They will be the first Congressional hearings on a handgun control measure in almost six years.

And Congressional opponents of the White House plan to abolish the Bureau of Alcohol, Tobacco and Firearms have already begun hearings to consider arguments that the bureau's enforcement functions should be transferred to the Justice Department, instead of the Secret Service.

"It's too early to tell which way things will go," Mr. Fraher said, "but I think if we can educate people on just what the McClure-Volkmer bill does, we have a chance of stopping it," at least in its present form.

Focus of Gun-Control Fight Shifts

BY FRANCIS X. CLINES | JUNE 7, 1982

THE NATION'S CHRONIC debate over gun controls, already burnished by cycles of time, tragedy and rhetoric into a Capitol Hill specialty, is waxing once again.

This time it is spurred by such factors as the wounding of a President, relentless new lobbying and some grisly doggerel from John W. Hinckley Jr., President Reagan's assailant. And this time, the legislative contest has begun with an unexpected setback for the National Rifle Association.

The association's own major legislative goal for this year, a bill designed to roll back many restrictions of the 1968 Gun Control Act, was quietly adopted by the Senate Judiciary Committee several weeks ago but with the unexpected inclusion of a key new control sought by Senator Edward M. Kennedy, Democrat of Massachusetts. His amendment would mandate a period of two weeks during which a potential purchaser of a pistol would have to wait for a search of criminal records.

PROPONENTS ARE PLEASED

Proponents, calling this the "Hinckley precaution," which might have snared Mr. Reagan's assailant before the shooting and after his earlier weapons arrest, are delighted at their success in committee. They say this is the first significant legislative step for the issue since the shooting of George Wallace of Alabama renewed the debate in 1972. Since then, the Government's estimate of pistols in the nation has roughly doubled, to 55 million, with 100 million predicted by the turn of the century, enough for one out of three Americans.

The Kennedy amendment is odious enough to the rifle association, which controls the gun lobby, so that the organization is now opposing its own amended bill as "emasculated." It is gearing up for a fight against the amendment on the Senate floor that its new lobbyist, J. Warren Cassidy, concedes will involve a risky public staking of prestige.

HE EXPECTS GROUP WILL RECOUP

"We were surprised by the committee action, no doubt about it," said Mr. Cassidy, who disputes the committee's voting procedure and insists his lobbying team will recoup on the floor. The committee's vote of 8 to 5 included in the affirmative Senator Charles E. Grassley, an Iowa Republican who is one of the leading beneficiaries of the association's donations for political candidates. This is because the amended bill presents something of a political crazyquilt for both sides. For example, Senator Kennedy is still opposed to the overall measure's weakening of the existing law, but senses he has a stronger bargaining position.

Mr. Cassidy, a 52-year-old former Mayor of Lynn, Mass., is a successful veteran of the fight against a ban on pistols in Massachusetts. He represents a new public voice in Washington for the association, whose board purged three of its top Washington officials in April amid conditions that still are not clear but that reportedly involved strategy in dealing with allies in the White House that backfired.

"The Hinckley case actually can work for us, other than that first emotional thrust in the press," Mr. Cassidy said in discussing the Senate bill, which is expected to be reported on to the floor calendar in a week or two. "Once people understand how existing gunlaw waiting periods don't work, and once they see all the debate by psychiatrists in our courts compared to other countries' handling of the Pope and Sadat shootings, and how Bobby Kennedy's killer was almost out again, we can make a strong case that the problem is not the tool at all but the criminal justice system."

TESTIMONY AT TRIAL CITED

In contrast, the new fast growing antipistol lobby, Handgun Control Inc., says it feels the Hinckley trial is providing the most classic dissection yet of an alarming trend in which stress-worn Americans find pistols ever more available. Such a trend, in the words of Charles Orasin, the organization's executive vice president, lets "the gunfight replace the fistfight."

In seven years of lobbying, Handgun Control claims 700,000 enlisted supporters. Its program focuses on dividing the rifle association's turf by drawing a distinction between the long-gun sportsmen and the wielders of pistols. The pistol-wielders, according to Government data, now account for more than 10,000 homicides a year, half the national total. The group lobbies Congress with a weekly statistical tattoo of victims and political subdivisions (an American dies by pistol every 55 minutes). Mr. Orasin says that beyond this, the revelations of the Hinckley trial, a few blocks from the Capitol, provide the most dramatic lobbying yet against the wayward passion for pistols. He cites such trial exhibits as Mr. Hinckley's verse, "Guns Are Fun!" which begins:

> See that living legend over there?
> With one little squeeze of the trigger
> I can put that person at my feet
> moaning and groaning and pleading with God.
> This gun gives me pornographic power.
> If I wish, the President will fall
> and the world will look at me in disbelief
> All because I own an inexpensive gun.

"Talk about a glaring example," said Mr. Orasin.

Mr. Cassidy, however, contends this is an emotional appeal, not a rational one and that the periodic fluctuations of the gun control issue only serve to strengthen the rifle association, whose membership is approaching 2.5 million members.

"We hurt any time a national figure is hurt like that," he said. "But what happens, Kennedy and the others jump up crying gun control and that awakens our people in the field so that contributions and new memberships come in: 30,000 more a month for the past 50 months. We must be doing something right."

Controls on Guns Supported in Polls

BY THE NEW YORK TIMES | JUNE 20, 1983

A MAJORITY OF AMERICANS favor stricter controls on pistol sales but stop short of calling for an outright ban, according to a Gallup Poll released yesterday.

The researchers reported that 59 percent favored stricter laws on the sales. Only 44 percent, however, favored a ban on the sale and possession of pistols, while 48 percent opposed such a ban.

In Gallup surveys dating to 1975, a majority have always favored stricter controls. The results over the years have been uneven, however. In 1975 the survey found 69 percent favoring stricter controls; in 1980 it was 59 percent and in 1982 it was 65 percent.

FEW WANT TO EASE LAWS

A very small minority of those questioned has favored less strict controls. This year that figure was 4 percent. Thirty-one percent said the laws should be kept as is, while 6 percent offered no opinion.

The 4 percent who felt that gun control laws should be less strict said that people needed guns to protect themselves and their property. They said that there was a Constitutional right to bear arms and that controls were not effective. Some said they wanted to keep their guns because they were hunters.

President Reagan has consistently said that pistol controls have not been effective. After John W. Hinckley Jr. wounded him in a 1981 assassination attempt with a pistol, Mr. Reagan said the laws had been no help in deterring the attack.

"Some of the stiffest gun laws are here in the District," the President said later, "and they didn't seem to prevent that fellow from carrying on down by the Hilton Hotel."

SOME OPPONENTS CONVINCED

The survey reported a widespread feeling, however, that stricter gun controls would reduce crime and deaths resulting from family arguments.

"Even significant proportions of Americans who oppose tougher handgun controls concede that such laws would reduce crime and prevent gun deaths," George Gallup, the director of the survey, said in reporting the results. "Many gun owners, as well, grant that tougher laws would contribute toward these desirable goals."

In general, the survey found that residents of cities with populations over 50,000 favored bans on the sale and possession of pistols, while those living in smaller cities and rural areas did not. The researchers reported that in cities with populations of one million or more the response was nearly 2 to 1 in favor of banning pistols. Support for a ban was about evenly divided in cities of 50,000 to 500,000 population and strongly opposed in communities below 50,000 and in rural areas.

MORE SUPPORT FROM WOMEN

Women responding to the poll favored a community ban on pistols by a margin of 15 percentage points. Men opposed such a ban by a margin of 25 points.

In addition, the poll found, a pistol ban is favored by those 18 to 24 years old, by white-collar workers and Easterners. It is opposed by persons 30 and older, those whose education ended at the high school level or earlier, blue-collar workers and non-Easterners.

There has been a sharp increase in the number of people who want guns for themselves. In New York City, for example, 9,268 applications were filed for pistol licenses last year — almost 1,000 more than the year before and more than twice the number before the State Legislature passed a tougher pistol law in 1980.

MIXED RESULTS IN COURT

Attempts to pass stricter controls on pistols have had mixed results.

Last October the California Court of Appeal overturned a San Francisco law that generally banned the possession of pistols on the ground that the city had no authority to enact it. But a law enacted in the Chicago suburb of Morton Grove, Ill., prohibiting the sale and private possession of pistols has withstood legal challenges.

Last November, Californians defeated a statewide ballot initiative that would have placed stronger controls on pistols. The initiative would have required the registration of pistols, prohibited their sale through the mails, mandated a six-month jail sentence for anyone carrying an unregistered pistol and restricted the future sale of such guns to those in law enforcement.

Gun Show a Weapons Supermarket

BY WAYNE KING | JUNE 28, 1985

THERE WAS EVERYTHING from .50-caliber machine guns, which require Federal clearance to purchase, to kits to make a .30-caliber Gatling gun, which almost anyone could buy, to an array of military-style assault weapons.

There were shotguns, rifles, handguns, crossbows, blowguns, kung fu throwing stars and fighting sticks, brass knuckles, 50,000-volt electric "stun guns," daggers, rapiers, sabers, parts, plans, kits and books to convert semiautomatic weapons into machine guns — even a kit of chemicals to make 20-odd gallons of napalm.

Every year there are several hundred to perhaps a thousand gun shows, and they are veritable supermarkets of weapons. At the one this weekend sponsored by the Dallas Arms Collectors Association, hundreds of dealers and private collectors filled 1,700 tables at Market Hall here.

Such shows, which are growing in number and size across the country, are both a testament to America's fascination with weapons and the source of a growing concern for gun control advocates.

The shows are generally organized by gun clubs or others who zealously defend what they maintain is every American's right to keep and bear arms. As a result dealers and private exhibitors maintain the most liberal interpretation of weapons laws.

CONVERSION KITS FOR SALE

Thus such shows, as in Dallas, will house display tables offering for sale semiautomatic assault-style weapons like the military M-1 and M-16 rifles, or the M-16's civilian version, the AR-15, all of which can be purchased by anyone who can legally buy a hunting rifle, side by side with other tables offering parts, plans, kits and manuals to convert these weapons to fully automatic machine guns.

A machine gun can be bought only by a person who has been fingerprinted and holds a permit in the form of a $200 tax stamp issued by the Treasury Department. So anyone seeking to avoid buying the tax stamp, and being fingerprinted and letting it be known he has the gun, can do so by buying a semiautomatic weapon and the kit to convert it.

Earlier this month, the Federal Government began to crack down on such illegal conversions by charging two companies in California and Georgia with conspiring to violate Federal gun laws.

According to John C. Killorin, chief of the public affairs branch of the Bureau of Alcohol, Tobacco and Firearms, the indictments culminated a yearlong investigation into allegations that the companies and their officers were involved in a scheme to market kits and parts from which machine guns and illegal silencers could be assembled.

INVESTIGATION CONTINUES

"We are alleging that one company manufactured some part, another the rest, and the parts were advertised and sold with the knowledge that they could and were in fact being illegally assembled," said Stephen E. Higgins, the director of the bureau.

In that case, the allegations dealt specifically with parts to assemble silencers, but the bureau is also continuing its investigation into the manufacture and marketing of conversion kits to turn semiautomatic weapons into machine guns.

At one booth at the Dallas gun show, a conversion kit for a MAC-10 semiautomatic weapon, which is easily and often converted to a machine gun, was offered for $75.

When the dealer was told a similar kit was offered at a Mississippi gun show a month earlier for $30, he replied, "Well, they're getting scarce — this is the last one I've got."

Another problem arising at gun shows, according to Art Agnos, a California Assemblyman, is that exhibitors at such shows who are not dealers fall into the category of private collectors. People in that category can sell handguns and other weapons without requiring the purchaser to fill out the firearms form required for a purchase from a dealer.

PISTOL SOLD TO FELON

Last month at a gun show in Stockton, Calif., Mr. Agnos, paying in cash and without providing any identification, bought a .32-caliber Berreta automatic pistol identical to one that was used to shoot him in 1973, in a wave of random violence known as the Zebra attacks that included 14 murders and seven armed assaults.

While Mr. Agnos was buying that weapon, another man, a convicted felon, used $150 the Assemblyman provided him to buy another automatic pistol at another table.

Neither man was asked to provide a driver's license or to provide any other form of identification.

It is illegal to sell a firearm to a convicted felon. In this case the buyer, who has served prison terms for armed robbery, possession of a sawed-off shotgun and assaulting a police officer, signed a false name to a statement that he had not been convicted of a crime, but he was not asked to provide proof of identity.

BILL WOULD LIMIT SALES

As a result of the incident, Mr. Agnos has introduced a bill that would require all handgun sales in California to be made through a dealer, with a mandatory 15-day waiting period and background check.

A companion bill would ban the sale, transfer or possession of any semiautomatic "military assault weapons" such as the AR-15, the M-16 and similar weapons, including the semiautomatic Uzi, the Israeli assault weapon originally designed as a machine gun, which can be restored to that mode with conversion kits that are readily available.

Such legislation is hotly opposed by gun advocates, and their attitude is reflected in posters and T-shirts for sale at gun shows like the one in Dallas this weekend.

"Gun Control," says one T-shirt, "Is Being Able to Hit Your Target."

Another, displaying a silenced Uzi submachine gun, bears the legend "The Whisper of Authority."

A poster warns, "If you are found here at night, you will be found here in the morning."

And another T-shirt urges, "Join the Marines. Travel to exotic, distant lands. Meet exciting, unusual people. And kill them." As for the proliferation of gun shows, which are organized by gun fanciers and hobbyists, Mr. Killorin said that the bureau investigated any complaints of abuses but did not monitor the shows as a routine matter.

"We are interested in guns going to criminals," he said. "We do not expend resources in fishing expeditions at gun shows."

Police Groups Reverse Stand and Back Controls on Pistols

BY JOHN HERBERS | OCT. 27, 1985

IN A SHARP DEPARTURE from the past, the nation's major police associations are fighting for controls on pistols, adding a new element to the long, bitter struggle over regulation of firearms.

The police lobby has been active in recent months at both the national and state levels and is currently pitted against the National Rifle Association in opposition to a bill before Congress to reduce Federal regulation of interstate gun sales.

In the past, the nation's law-enforcement officers remained mostly in the background on issues related to gun control. While some big-city police chiefs testified for more controls, much of the rank and file, according to all accounts, embraced many of the goals of the rifle association, the chief lobby opposing controls. Police influence on legislation was therefore muted.

An example of the change is provided by the Fraternal Order of Police, which says it has 170,000 members in 43 states. Its national president, Richard A. Boyd of Oklahoma City, said that a few years ago the union supported the National Rifle Association in its efforts to roll back controls contained in the Federal Gun Control Act of 1968.

DISPUTE OVER BULLETS

Now, however, the police group is actively opposing those efforts, in a coalition with the National Sheriffs Association, the International Association of Chiefs of Police, the National Organization of Black Law Enforcement Executives, the National Troopers Association and two research and policy groups, the Police Executive Research Forum and the Police Foundation.

Mr. Boyd said one factor in the turnaround was the rifle association's opposition to legislation that would ban armor-piercing bullets, which are said to have caused the death of some police officers. The Federal legislation, sponsored by Representative Mario Biaggi, Democrat of the Bronx, was defeated last year under the intense lobbying of the rifle association, which opposes virtually all governmental controls on firearms. The experience left many police officers "embittered toward the N.R.A.," Mr. Boyd said.

G. Ray Arnett, executive vice president of the rifle association, wrote a letter to law-enforcement officers this summer to explain his organization's opposition to the Biaggi bill. "Legislation that is unenforceable and generated solely to gain headlines or to make 'political points' is bad legislation," he said. "It offers no protection to law enforcement or the public."

STATES PROVIDE A FORUM

The issue also arose in some state legislatures where the police and gun lobbies again fought, but with the police lobby scoring some victories.

Fourteen states have passed bills similar to the Biaggi measure, Mr. Boyd said in an interview. And the proposal has been revived in Congress, again with police support.

States in the Northeast with large urban populations, including New York, New Jersey and Connecticut, have long had laws restricting the sale and transportation of firearms. Now, with police support, pressure for more controls has been spreading to other parts of the country.

In South Carolina, for example, a coalition of law-enforcement officers sponsored a bill in the Legislature this year to require a waiting period and background check before a gun can be sold. It was defeated, in part by opposition from the National Rifle Association. But law-enforcement officials have succeeded in North Carolina and several other states.

Police groups also find themselves at odds with the rifle association in Massachusetts, where the association is pushing legislation to reduce police departments' discretion in denying pistol licenses. Governor Cuomo vetoed a similar bill in New York in 1982, and the California Legislature killed the same type of bill in 1983.

FOCUS ON INTERSTATE SALES

But the focus of the police lobby now is on the bill passed by the Senate last year to dilute the 1968 gun control law, which was enacted in the wake of the assassinations of the Rev. Dr. Martin Luther King Jr. and Senator Robert F. Kennedy. The revisions would make it easier for Americans to buy, sell and transport firearms, largely by making it legal to purchase a gun outside a purchaser's home state so long as the purchaser has a face-to-face meeting with the dealer and the transaction does not violate state law. Most interstate purchases are now prohibited.

Although the revision passed the Senate 79 to 15, it is opposed in the House by such Democratic leaders as Peter W. Rodino Jr. of New Jersey, the chairman of the Judiciary Committee. Sponsors of the measure, saying a majority of House members favor it, filed a petition Tuesday to bring the measure directly to the floor. If they gain the necessary 218 signatures, the bill will probably come to a vote in a few months, both sides said.

In the meantime, however, the Judiciary Subcommittee on Crime, headed by William J. Hughes, another New Jersey Democrat, has scheduled public hearings around the nation in which police officers will be prominent among the witnesses. The first hearing will be held in Manhattan, at the International Court of Trade, 1 Federal Plaza, at 9:30 A.M. tomorrow.

GUN CONTROL GROUPS' IMAGE

Established groups within the gun control lobby such as Handgun Control welcome the police pressures for reasons beyond the political influence of those in law enforcement. Over the years, they say, many people have associated the gun control lobby with liberal Democratic causes. The police, on the other hand, are widely considered part of the conservative, blue-collar middle class who cannot be accused of coddling criminals, as other supporters of controls were Tuesday on the floor of the House.

The police lobby's opposition to the measure coalesced after the Senate agreed to dilute the 1968 law. In a memorandum to House members, representatives of the police groups said they were concerned by statements made on the Senate floor that the bill had the support of law enforcers.

"To the contrary," they said, "we in the law-enforcement community are very disturbed with provisions of the bill that would permit face-to-face interstate sale of handguns. This, we firmly believe, would undermine state and local laws and make our job of protecting the public more difficult."

Jerald Vaughn, director of the International Association of Chiefs of Police, said: "We are imploring members of Congress, asking them not to turn the clock back. This bill will not help law enforcement. It will only create more problems."

RIFLE ASSOCIATION RESPONDS

"That is balderdash," said Denise Rosson, a spokesman for the National Rifle Association. She said the law enforcement officers had been "misinformed" and that the "rank and file" agreed with her organization. Both the Justice and Treasury Departments certified that the bill would not hurt local law enforcement, she added.

She also pointed out that the rifle association had enjoyed a close relation with police groups, that it provides gun training for 180,000 police officers and that some police groups support the association's legislative goals. She supplied the name of one organization, the American Federation of Police.

Gerald Orenberg of Miami, head of the federation, said his group was prevented by Federal tax laws from lobbying and that he had little knowledge of the issues. "But we support the N.R.A.," he added.

DISPUTE OVER MOTIVES

Mr. Boyd of the Fraternal Order of Police made it clear that many police officers thought the rifle association had gone too far toward opposition to any controls. "They are in this for the gun dealers," he said. "I don't know why."

The rifle association and Congressional supporters of the revisions deny this, saying that the regulations and paperwork have become too burdensome and that gun owners have been unjustly accused of violations.

Mr. Boyd said the disagreement over legislation did not amount to a break with the rifle association. "We still support them on the right to bear arms," he said, "and we are with them on opposing registration of guns."

CHAPTER 3

A Call for Greater Gun Control

Two major pieces of legislation in 1994 put limits on gun ownership. The Brady Handgun Violence Prevention Act — named after James Brady, who had been injured in the 1981 assassination attempt on President Reagan — imposed a five-day waiting period and background checks before the purchase of a gun, while the Violent Crime Control and Law Enforcement Act banned certain assault weapons. On April 20, 1999, two students at Columbine High School in Colorado killed 13 people, a tragedy that shocked the nation but did not inspire a new round of federal gun control efforts.

From One Woman's Tragedy, the Making of an Advocate

BY PETER MARKS | AUG. 18, 1994

SOMETIMES, LATE AT NIGHT, Carolyn McCarthy gets phone calls from strangers looking for arguments. The callers begin by offering their condolences, but soon the tone changes, and Mrs. McCarthy finds herself on the line with another person angry over her outspoken advocacy of gun control.

Mrs. McCarthy, whose husband was killed and whose son was seriously injured in the shooting last December aboard a Long Island Rail Road train that left six people dead, says she never hangs up on them. She stays on even when people become a little cruel, intimating

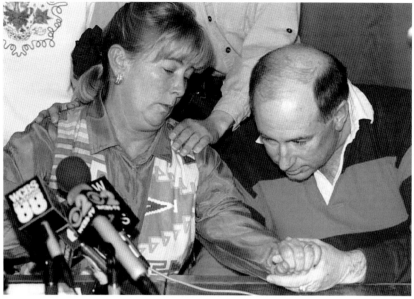

DON EMMERT/AFP/GETTY IMAGES

Carolyn McCarthy speaks at a news conference about her son's condition two days after he was wounded in a shooting in December 1993.

that her motives for appearing before the television cameras are less than pure.

"They'll say, 'You're quite an actress,' " Mrs. McCarthy recounted. "I don't answer back. I'll say, 'I'm sorry you feel that way. But hopefully what I'm doing might save your wife or son someday. Because we don't want anyone else to go through this.' "

Lately, Mrs. McCarthy has been in front of the cameras a lot. Whether lobbying in Washington for President Clinton's crime bill, or urging lawmakers in Albany to ban assault weapons, she is an increasingly visible figure in the debate over gun control. But nothing in recent months has given her more exposure than her decision to appear in a commercial for Gov. Mario M. Cuomo, a campaign ad that has raised her profile in New York and thrust her advocacy into the political arena.

Mrs. McCarthy said she had no second thoughts about appearing in the ad, which has been broadcast on New York stations for about

A CALL FOR GREATER GUN CONTROL **77**

a month. In fact, she said, she was irritated when, during a recent appearance with Mr. Cuomo in her Mineola home, reporters suggested that the Cuomo campaign was using her.

"To be used, you have to feel like you're being used," Mrs. McCarthy said. "I looked at it as, 'Who's using who?' "

A campaign aide to Mr. Cuomo called Mrs. McCarthy and asked her to make the commercial after she had appeared with the Governor at several events organized to muster public support for the ban on assault weapons. Mrs. McCarthy said she did not recall which aide approached her about the ad, which was partly filmed in her backyard and was made without a script.

"I didn't even have to think twice about it," she said, of her decision to appear in the commercial, adding that though she is a Republican, she felt such a kinship with the Democratic Governor on the assault-weapons issue that she had no doubts about the ad.

The commercial has become a centerpiece of the Cuomo campaign's efforts to portray him as tough on crime, and to answer Republican attacks on the Governor's vetoes of bills to reinstate the death penalty in New York. In the 60-second commercial, which was produced by David Garth, Mr. Cuomo's media adviser, Mrs. McCarthy and Thomas F. McDermott, a lawyer from Garden City who was wounded in the Dec. 7 shooting, praise Mr. Cuomo for his opposition to capital punishment and his support for an assault-weapons ban.

"Obviously, the tragedy of the railroad shooting was so shocking that I think people are really affected by what she has to say," Joel R. Benenson, a campaign spokesman, said of Mrs. McCarthy. "She's a very compelling personality."

In the eight months since the shooting, relatives and close friends have watched Mrs. McCarthy's evolution as an advocate with a mixture of admiration and awe. It is not a role she was born to: a nurse by training, Mrs. McCarthy had no previous experience in politics or public speaking. And she has had to juggle the demands of her new calling with the more emotionally demanding job of overseeing the recovery of her only child, Kevin, 27, who was left partly paralyzed as a result of the head wounds he sustained in the shooting.

WON'T SPEAK FOR MONEY

While the families of most of the other shooting victims have shied from publicity, Mrs. McCarthy said she feels compelled to agree to interviews and accept speaking engagements that she believes will advance her cause. She has rejected, however, all requests to speak for money, or to go on the Oprah-Montel-Sally Jessy circuit. "We got lots of flowers and chocolate chip cookie cakes from them," she said with a laugh.

Carol Neary, Mrs. McCarthy's closest friend, said that Mrs. McCarthy has always been the kind of person others turned to in an emergency. But even she was amazed at her friend's capacity to hold her emotions in check and speak extemporaneously to large groups.

"She was very shy when I met her years ago," she said. "She was more of a one-to-one person, not talking to a whole crowd. And all of sudden, there she was in front of the media, and it was just so natural to her. She seemed to be so natural, so comfortable."

Today, for the second time in a week, Mrs. McCarthy went to Washington, joining a large number of crime victims and their relatives who have been lobbying for the crime bill, which includes a provision to prohibit the sale of assault weapons. She and Mr. McDermott have visited the offices of several Representatives from Long Island, some of whom found it hard to look Mrs. McCarthy in the eye and explain why they were opposing the legislation.

"It was extremely hard to do it, but you absolutely had to do it," said Representative Peter T. King, a Republican from Seaford. The competition among lobbyists to get in to see Representatives is intense on an issue as hard fought as this one, but Mr. King said he felt a special obligation to hear Mrs. McCarthy and Mr. McDermott. "They're not professional advocates," he said. "They're coming from their hearts."

When Mrs. McCarthy speaks, she often mentions her opposition to the death penalty, a position that surprises some people. "I'm totally against it, and always have been," she said, sitting at the dining room table of her modest house, which is being renovated to accommodate her son's disabilities. "I think that's very hard for some people to understand. But I'm a nurse. I have been fighting all my life to save someone's life."

A FAST RECOVERY

Mr. McCarthy, released from a rehabilitation hospital in April in what his doctors described as a remarkably fast recovery, walks a bit stiffly and has limited use of his right hand, which was injured in the attack that killed his father, Dennis. But he is learning to drive again, his mother said, and is traveling by himself to Milwaukee soon.

Mrs. McCarthy says her son is the only person she consults before agreeing to speak. If he did not approve, her days in front of the cameras would probably come to an end. But that might not be an easy decision for her, because speaking out has helped her to feel she is doing something for her late husband.

"All the energy goes toward the gun control," she said. "That probably has been my release."

After Vigil for Verdict,
a Plea for Gun Control

BY THE NEW YORK TIMES | FEB. 18, 1995

IN AN EXTRAORDINARY courthouse press conference minutes after Colin Ferguson was convicted in the Long Island Rail Road shooting spree, survivors and relatives of those who died used their moments before the cameras to plead for stricter gun control, rather than to condemn Mr. Ferguson.

"The manufacturers, the gun people look for the almighty dollar," Robert Giugliano said, his voice rising. "Enough is enough."

Mr. Giugliano, who was shot in the chest and arms by Mr. Ferguson, seemed near tears as he spoke before scores of reporters and cameras.

The half-dozen people who gathered to speak after Mr. Ferguson was pronounced guilty of killing 6 and wounding 19 had clearly coordinated their prepared statements and planned their strategy to make a strong stand against gun manufacturers and their political supporters.

The speeches were all short, but carefully drawn. Tom McDermott began with the phrase "we the survivors of the L.I.R.R. 5:33." Arlene LoCicero opened with the comment, "I'm the mother of a murdered child." Her daughter, Amy Federici, was one of the six who died. The LoCiceros had donated their daughter's heart and kidneys, enabling three ill people from across the country to live.

Alluding to Mr. Ferguson, Mr. McDermott said, "Until 10 minutes ago he could have purchased the gun." He said that if Congress weakened Federal assault weapon laws, it will have "disgraced and dishonored the lives of the six human beings who never came off the car."

Mrs. LoCicero said, "The gun manufacturers are responsible for the advertising and making of their products."

The main spokeswoman for the victims, Carolyn McCarthy, whose husband was killed in the shooting and whose son nearly died, said,

"The gun manufacturers continue to advertise bullets that will tear away flesh."

Mrs. McCarthy told those gathered that "it's been a long 14 months, but justice has been done."

Her son, Kevin McCarthy, who had not been expected to survive and who lost 10 percent of his brain in subsequent surgery, spoke first last night. "It's been a long, hard road with many hurdles," he said. He started thanking people, naming individuals including Judge Donald Belfi and detectives, but then, when he could not remember the prosecutor's name, he stopped and looked down at his mother.

"George Peck," she said, smiling at him.

She broke down at one point and apologized to the gathered reporters. During questions, she was asked her feelings about Mr. Ferguson but said that now that the trial was over, she had put him out of her mind forever.

Toward the end of the press conference she thanked everyone, and in closing said, "You haven't heard the last of us."

Bush, Usually Opponent of Gun Control, Backs 2 Restrictions Proposed in Congress

BY DAVID STOUT | **AUG. 28, 1999**

WINDING UP A campaign fund-raising trip in a region stunned by recent bloodshed, Gov. George W. Bush of Texas said in Georgia today that he supported two gun-control measures that have been proposed in Congress.

The measures would outlaw the imports of certain high-capacity ammunition clips and raise the legal age to 21, from 18, for handgun purchases.

"Those are reasonable measures," Mr. Bush said in a brief question-and-answer session with journalists in Marietta.

Aides to the Governor, who is seeking the Republican Presidential nomination, said Mr. Bush's stance on those measures did not represent new thinking on gun control, which he generally opposes. Rather, they said, Mr. Bush was simply articulating views on specific issues that he had never been asked about before.

As if seeking to avoid the impression that his views on high-capacity clips and age requirements signal a wholesale shift in his philosophy, Mr. Bush said, "I believe innocent people, law-abiding citizens, ought to be allowed to own a gun."

The Governor has signed laws expanding the right of Texans to carry guns, and last spring he signed a law that bars Texas cities from suing the gun industry.

Gun control has been a heated issue in recent months, after several bloody incidents across the country. Three of them occurred in Georgia. On July 29, a securities day-trader shot and killed nine people, then himself, in Atlanta. On July 12, a gunman in Atlanta killed two women and four children before taking his own life. And on May 20, a 15-year-old boy opened fire at his school in Conyers, Ga., wounding six classmates.

The measures Mr. Bush backed today enjoy considerable support among Republicans and Democrats. In May, the Senate endorsed several gun-control measures, including curbs on importing high-capacity ammunition clips, although it took no action on the age-ownership issue.

But the House was unable to agree on gun control, in part because conservative lawmakers found some of the measures too restrictive and liberal lawmakers found some too lenient. The issue is certain to be resurrected when Congress returns from recess in September.

On an issue that divides Republicans and Democrats, requiring all vendors at gun shows to conduct background checks of prospective buyers, Mr. Bush has taken his party's position. Republicans generally favor a rule that such checks be completed within 24 hours; Democrats would allow three business days. (Federally licensed dealers at gun shows must now do background checks, and they have three business days to do so.)

Mr. Bush also sought today to differentiate his and Vice President Al Gore's positions on government aid to religious organizations that do social-service work.

Mr. Gore, who is seeking the Democratic Presidential nomination, has said he opposes any proselytizing by such organizations. Mr. Bush said that, while government should assist the programs rather than the churches or synagogues that run them, "we ought to understand the power of the message" of the institutions.

A Gun Control Moment

EDITORIAL | BY THE NEW YORK TIMES | APRIL 28, 1999

THE COLORADO SCHOOL massacre has generated what amounts to a national conversation about causes and cures, raising issues as simple as school security, as delicate as parental responsibility and as complex as the biological and cultural roots of teen-age violence. This discussion could well lead to a more alert and safer society. But there is one blindingly obvious issue that should be addressed right away — the issue of gun control. Congress, nervous about the gun lobby, is divided on the subject. The public, we suspect, is not divided at all, at least on the matter of keeping guns and explosives out of the hands of young people. Our own view is that the Colorado tragedy has provided the right moment to take the issue of gun control off automatic pilot, where it has been for four years, and move it forward in a dramatic way.

President Clinton seems to have sensed that such a moment may be at hand, that the country may be at one of those rare turning points where the weight of public shock and anger creates the necessary conditions for major legislative change. Yesterday he offered a solid package of gun control measures. The package — a mixture of old measures ignored by Congress and several new initiatives — offers no guarantee against a repetition of the Colorado horror. No law can do that. What these measures would do is reduce the risk by making it harder for disturbed young people to obtain guns and explosives.

Such change will not come easy in this Congress. The Republican leaders, House Speaker Dennis Hastert and the Senate majority leader, Trent Lott, have expressed their wish for a national forum on "youth and culture," a clear indication that they would prefer to talk about anything other than gun control. The Democrats, many of whom attribute their Congressional losses in 1994 to that year's vote to ban assault weapons, seem equally skittish. "I'm not sure that gun control is what we need," declared their leader in the Senate, Tom

Daschle, who preferred to dilate about violence on the Internet and in the media.

Yet Mr. Clinton's package is one around which the public and Congress, if it will only open its eyes and ears, can usefully rally. Its key elements deserve thorough debate and an up-or-down vote in both houses of Congress by mid-summer. We can think of no better legislative gift to the students who will be returning to school next fall.

Several provisions are aimed at closing off the ways that young people now lay their hands on weapons. One would raise the minimum age for possessing handguns to 21. Federal law prohibits Federally licensed gun dealers from selling handguns to anyone under 21, but allows 18- to 20-year-olds to possess handguns and even to buy them from unlicensed sellers, such as an older friend, which may be how the Colorado shooters obtained some of their arsenal. Another proposal would ban juvenile possession of semiautomatic assault rifles, as well as imports of high-capacity ammunition clips.

A third provision would hold parents criminally liable when they "knowingly or recklessly" allow a child access to a weapon that later causes death or injury. Sixteen states already have such laws, and they have helped reduce violence. A fourth provision would require dealers, manufacturers and importers to provide a child safety lock with every gun. This proposal could be strengthened by requiring that the locks be pre-installed at the factory. Congress could go a step further by underwriting "smart gun" technology to prevent the firing of weapons by people other than authorized users.

The President also recommended updating the 1993 Brady law, which requires a background check of handgun buyers and has prevented more than a quarter of a million felons from obtaining handguns. Mr. Clinton would extend the Brady background check to the sale of explosives, and close a big loophole that allows people to evade a check by buying guns at gun shows or flea markets. At the same time, Congress needs to plug another loophole identified by Senator Charles Schumer of New York, by prohibiting gun sales over the Internet.

Mr. Clinton endorsed for the first time the notion of limiting individual gun purchases to one a month — an antidote, already in effect in some states, to illegal traffickers who make bulk purchases in states with weak gun control laws and then sell guns to youngsters in states with strong laws, like New York.

This is a big package. But this is the right time to push it. The National Rifle Association is at least temporarily on the run, in the states and in the courts. And the public is eager for change.

Politics Among Culprits in Death of Gun Control

BY ALISON MITCHELL | JUNE 19, 1999

FOR ALL THE national horror at the carnage in Littleton, Colo., the sentiment could not keep gun-control legislation from collapsing on the House floor. All that was left this afternoon was a cloud of dust and a bitter political debate over who killed gun control in the House.

The confounding outcome was the result of a number of factors, including the narrow majority of House Republicans, the sway of conservatives over the Republican caucus, the determination of Democrats to win back the House in 2000 and the differing views in both parties on how the gun issue will play on Election Day.

Only an extremely strong leader might have been able to navigate such crosscurrents. But Speaker J. Dennis Hastert of Illinois was little seen, having said he would let members do as they wished. He even left it up to Representative Tom DeLay of Texas, the majority whip, and Representative J. C. Watts Jr. of Oklahoma, the fourth-ranking leader, to try to explain to reporters what happened today. (They blamed the Democrats.)

In any event, the passage of something as emotional as gun control would have taken good will between the parties. But that disappeared in the days of impeachment.

As charges and countercharges flew, Representative Carolyn McCarthy of Long Island, who went to Congress after her husband was killed by a gunman on the Long Island Rail Road, said, "This is not a game to me." Near tears on the House floor at 1 A.M., she said, "This is not a game to the American people."

But political games were indeed being played by all sides.

The groundwork for today's outcome was laid when Mr. Hastert spoke out for some small steps for gun control after the Senate's surprise passage of modest gun-control measures. He described his position as his personal opinion. But his remarks left it clear that House Republicans wanted to avoid looking as tone-deaf and defensive as Senate Republicans did when they considered gun control last month.

So House Republican leaders then tried to assemble a gun-control bill that conservatives could embrace.

Working with Representative John D. Dingell, a Michigan Democrat who is an avid supporter of gun rights, they drafted a proposal to regulate gun shows that was blessed by the National Rifle Association. It was not only the most lenient of several competing gun-show provisions to come to the House floor for consideration, according to Democrats, it also weakened current gun laws. Mr. Dingell's measure would have granted 24 hours for background checks to be completed on buyers at gun shows by licensed dealers and hobbyists. But under current law licensed dealers have three business days to complete a background check for such sales.

The Dingell amendment passed with the support of most Republicans, including some conservatives who would normally vote against any gun-control measure. And it drew the allegiance of 45 conservative Democrats, primarily from Southern and Western districts whose constituents embrace gun rights.

But the passage of Mr. Dingell's measure and the subsequent defeat of Mrs. McCarthy's more stringent amendment left many Democrats determined to oppose the final bill, rather than allow the Republicans to say they had made a modest step on gun control. "Morally I cannot vote for it, because it does set us back," Mrs. McCarthy said.

The Republicans gave such Democrats reasons to vote for the bill, and a few more reasons to oppose it.

The House approved an amendment requiring safety locks to be sold with handguns and another banning the import of high-capacity ammunition clips. But it also weakened District of Columbia gun laws by voting to allow residents with no criminal history to possess loaded handguns in their homes. And Republicans blocked any House vote on a measure that would have raised the minimum age for all handgun purchases to 21 from 18.

In response, all but 10 Democrats opposed the bill en masse — choosing to have a campaign issue against the Republicans rather than a very modest gun-control measure.

President Clinton himself immediately began the Democratic campaign refrain saying, "This week, instead of listening to the American people and strengthening our gun laws, the House of Representatives listened to the gun lobby and did nothing at all."

The Democratic rebellion meant that to pass the legislation virtually all Republicans would have had to vote for it. Mr. Hastert had originally called gun control a "vote of conscience" and said Republicans would let members do as they wished. While he stood back Mr. DeLay rallied conservatives to support Mr. Dingell's measure but left it ambiguous whether he would vote for the final bill. (He did.)

Then today, just a few hours before the vote, Republican leaders met and the Speaker called for an all-out effort to pass the bill, Republicans said. Mr. Hastert even appeared today before Republican moderates to seek their vote.

But 82 Republicans broke with their party to vote against the bill. Some were moderates like Representative Marge Roukema of New Jersey, who had co-sponsored Mrs. McCarthy's measure, and Representative Tom Campbell of California, who tried to help Democrats today by bringing to the floor speaker after speaker whom he introduced as a "reasonable Republican for reasonable gun control."

Also voting against the bill were a number of Southern and Midwestern conservatives who are proud supporters of the Second Amendment's right to bear arms and were opposed to any gun control.

"What we did was ultimately craft a bill that nobody was pleased with," said Representative Bob Riley, an Alabama Republican who voted against the measure, saying it contained too much gun regulation.

Most Republicans, however, focused on the Democrats in explaining the outcome.

"It is quite obvious to me that they are just interested in politics," Mr. DeLay said, "not interested in even getting what they could get with the votes that were available to be had."

How gun control will ultimately affect the battle for the House is uncertain. It was once thought that gun-rights advocates were a potent single-issue voting bloc while gun control supporters did not turn out at the polls with the same intensity.

And many Republicans — who won the House majority in 1994 with help from the N.R.A. — believe that this political maxim still holds true.

Some gleeful Republican strategists said today that several Democrats from conservative regions of the country had cast a vote that would come back to haunt them when they stood with their party on the Dingell amendment. They named Representatives Bart Stupak and David E. Bonior of Michigan, Bob Etheridge of North Carolina and Collin C. Peterson of Minnesota as Democrats whom they would try to tar as gun-control zealots in 2000.

Democrats argued that the school shootings had changed the political equation since 1994 and that fearful suburban parents would emerge as a political counterforce to the N.R.A.

"It used to be a one-sided issue," said Representative Barney Frank, Democrat of Massachusetts. "Now it's a two-sided issue."

Democrats noted that many of the most hotly contested House seats are now suburban and that suburbanites turn out strongly in Presidential election years. But Mr. Frank acknowledged that it was hard to judge now whether voters would be thinking about school shootings in 18 months.

"Nobody is running for office tomorrow or next week," he said. "They are running for office in November of 2000. If it will still have the immediacy, nobody knows."

Towns Learn Banning Guns Is Not Easy

BY JACQUELINE BENNETT | DEC. 12, 1999

NOT LONG AFTER a disgruntled worker killed four people, then himself, at the Connecticut Lottery headquarters in Newington and after several school shootings around the nation in 1998, the General Assembly passed a law that prohibits the possession of all weapons on school grounds. The Assembly also gave municipalities the right to enact legislation that would ban weapons from town property.

Since then, several towns and cities around the state have weighed such a ban, but with little success. Windsor proposed the ban, but many residents at a public meeting last year said they were against it. A town councilman in West Hartford proposed a ban in August, but the council has yet to vote on it. In East Hartford, a similar proposal is being studied by a town council comittee.

But the gun bans are controversial, and no matter where they are contemplated, they have raised strong feelings.

"People were shocked," said Robert Fortier, a Republican town councilman in East Hartford who lost his bid for mayor in last month's election. "They don't want their rights messed with."

Kevin Searles, the police chief of Windsor, said under current state law, gun owners may carry a licensed firearm anywhere it is not prohibited, such as schools and the State Capitol building. The gun can even be concealed.

In East Hartford, the proposal for a gun ban was made by Steven Karlson, a Democrat on the town council. It has been sent to the council's ordinance committee for further consideration.

"Thousands of children use our parks and libraries as well as take part in recreational programs each year," he said. "I see no reason for anyone to carry a deadly weapon in our facilities especially when children are using those grounds.

"I'm a licensed owner" he added, pointing out that he rarely carries his gun at all.

Opponents have dubbed the proposal "feel-good legislation" and charge it plays on people's fears over recent shootings around the country.

Mr. Fortier said he sometimes carried a licensed gun for protection on evening walks by a dike in a remote part of town. He sees the ban as an infringement on his rights and worries where it could lead.

"If they start with town property, what do they do next?" he said.

Mr. Karlson said the issue went beyond the right to carry firearms, to the appropriateness of carrying weapons "into certain situations." Besides, he said, the town police can protect the public.

"We have 126 sworn officers in East Hartford," he said. "I would hate to say people need to carry weapons for self-defense."

Richard Kehoe, the Democrat who is chairman of the East Hartford town council, said that if the committee voted to send the proposed ban back to the council for action, it would have to go to a public hearing before the council could adopt it as an ordinance.

"Intuitively, I cannot understand why there is a need to carry a weapon on town property" he said.

Mayor Timothy Larson of East Hartford, a Democrat, supports the ban and said he believed it was important for town leaders to make a statement about their feelings about guns.

Ralph Sherman of Waterbury, the chairman of Gunsafe, a Connecticut group that supports the Second Amendment, called the East Hartford ban an invitation for criminals to target the town, aware that people would be prohibited from carrying weapons on town property. If East Hartford denies people the civil right of self-defense, the town is liable, he said. According to the Connecticut State Police, about 140,000 firearms permits are currently issued by the state.

Mr. Sherman won a State Superior Court ruling in April challenging a hunting ban in East Hartford. The town is appealing. He is bothered by increasing restrictions on gun ownership, what he calls "the chipping away of civil rights."

He also opposes a gun ban that was proposed in West Hartford by a town councilman. That proposal, by John Shulansky, a Democrat, was made in August after the shooting of children at a Jewish Community Center in California and an order from Governor John Rowland last summer barring state employees from bringing weapons to work. Mr. Shulansky's proposal has not made it to committee or a public hearing, but the Republican-controlled West Hartford town council did pass a resolution calling for a security audit of town buildings.

Mr. Shulansky, a vice president of IBP Aerospace Group of East Hartford, has been appealing to officials in other towns to adopt a weapons ban. He "urged" Mr. Karlson to propose the ban in East Hartford.

"I've always been a little concerned with the prevalence of guns in our society. I think it's the right thing to do," Mr. Shulansky said of the ban.

Robert Bouvier, the Republican mayor of West Hartford, opposes the ban proposed by Mr. Shulansky and said other ways should be found to deal with the problem, such as a town policy that does not allow old police guns to be sold to wholesalers, decreasing the chances they will reach the wrong hands.

In Windsor, town officials sent the gun proposal back to committee. Timothy Curtis, the deputy mayor, said he did not see the ban as a genuine deterrent. He said a ban would give the wrong impression that Windsor had experienced problems with weapons. Mr. Curtis said he planned to ask members of the council's Health and Safety Committee to decide whether to send the gun ban issue back to the council or to drop it.

"It was more of a statement than a deterrent," he said of the proposed ban.

James Manown, a spokesman for the National Rifle Association, said the Second Amendment protects law-abiding citizens' rights to own and use firearms.

The debate over gun control is also heating up elsewhere. Kevin Sullivan, Democrat of West Hartford and president pro tempore of the Senate, said he might propose, through one of the legislative committees in the February session, a ban on weapons in all public buildings in the state.

And in Greenwich, the police used a law that took effect Oct. 1 to take weapons and ammunition from a resident after a neighbor complained. Other towns have also seized guns under the law, which allows police to take weapons if the owners are believed to be a threat to the community.

George Jepsen of Stamford, the State Senate majority leader, said the state laws were more a response to the "broader spectrum of violence" in the United States rather than to specific occurrences here. But he said incidents like drive-by shootings a few years ago created a "climate ripe" for legislators to support the measures. Mr. Jepsen said the laws put Connecticut right where he wants the state to be, "trying to pursue the edge of the envelope on gun control."

State Representative Richard Tulisano, a Democrat from Rocky Hill, opposes the new law and said he plans to propose its repeal or modification in the February legislative session. He believes the law violates privacy rights.

"We've come a long way from the Founding Fathers," Mr. Tulisano said.

Mr. Bouvier of West Hartford said he doesn't think gun bans work.

"I don't want to give residents a false sense of security," he said, "to make them think there's no need to worry about guns falling into the wrong hands, that Columbine couldn't happen in West Hartford."

Statements Put White House Into a Gun Control Debate

BY NEIL A. LEWIS | OCT. 17, 2002

THE WHITE HOUSE found itself embroiled today in a combination of volatile gun control politics and the public's anxiety over the sniper in the Washington area.

Ari Fleischer, the White House spokesman, told reporters that the announcement on Tuesday evening of Mr. Bush's interest in exploring whether a so-called ballistic fingerprinting system should be implemented nationwide was not a marked departure for the president. Earlier on Tuesday, Mr. Fleischer said the president had doubts about the technological feasibility of such a system.

Mr. Fleischer had been asked the president's views on such a system, which some had said could have helped the police track down a serial killer who has killed nine people in the Washington area in the last two weeks.

To gun control advocates and ballistics experts, it appeared that the White House had erred with Mr. Fleischer's earlier statement raising questions about the idea's reliability. They noted that the system had been widely tested and had the support of many present and former government specialists in the Bureau of Alcohol, Tobacco and Firearms. Moreover, they said, it seemed the White House was being reflexively dismissive of something that was opposed by the gun rights lobby but that experts have said might have helped break the case of the sniper.

Joe Vince, a former agent with the firearms bureau who helped develop the system, said today, "This technology has been tested across the world and has shown itself to be highly effective."

Mr. Vince, who served with the bureau for 29 years and ended up as its chief of crime gun analysis, said it was imperative that law enforcement agencies, especially local police departments, have access to a nationwide computerized system of ballistics identification.

The debate concerns a system in which any new handgun that is sold would have a test round fired from its chamber and sent to the firearms bureau so its fingerprint — the unique marks that guns leave on bullets — would be recorded in a centralized database.

Currently, the bureau tracks only bullets and casings found at crime scenes. That means that the police can tell only whether bullet fragments or shell casings found at a crime scene match another crime scene bullet and determine if they came from the same gun. This is how the authorities determined that the 11 shootings in the Washington area were from the same weapon.

But in a system in which all new guns had their fingerprints on file, the authorities could simply match an individual bullet to the database and determine who originally bought the gun as well as where and when.

The National Rifle Association has vigorously opposed bullet fingerprinting, likening it to gun registration, which the group staunchly opposes. Andrew Rulanaudam, a spokesman for the association, declined to comment or even discuss the group's previously stated position on ballistic fingerprinting.

Mr. Vince said: "This is not a gun control issue. It's a public safety issue. Law enforcement has to have 21st-century technology to operate in today's society."

Only the states of New York and Maryland have bullet fingerprinting systems. When a gun is sold, the box usually contains test rounds fired by the manufacturer, and the gun dealer is required to send those bullets to the state police. A Canadian company has developed a computer that records an image of those bullets, which may be matched against any bullet that comes in from a crime scene.

Experts have said that if such a system had been in place it could have advanced the investigation of the sniper in the Washington area since the only pieces of evidence available for days were bullet fragments.

Amy Stilwell, a spokesman for the Brady Center to Prevent Gun Violence, a gun control group in Washington, said, "By the evening the

White House was trying to walk down its position without stating its real views."

Ms. Stilwell said that calling for a study "is a tried and true tactic to dispel public criticism while delaying the issue."

Opponents of the system say it would be ineffective because markings change slightly each time a gun is fired, making matches over time difficult, if not impossible. They also say it would be of little use for stolen guns, which are often used in crimes.

Senator Tom Daschle of South Dakota, the Democratic leader, said today that the shootings in the Washington area should oblige Congress to consider legislation that has been stalled calling for ballistic fingerprinting.

"I think the special interests, once again, seem to have the upper hand when it comes to these legislative opportunities," Mr. Daschle said. "The law enforcement community has looked at this legislation and, I think, universally and virtually unanimously have supported this legislation. Now, here we are in the throes of one of the most serious threats to this community, to this area that we've seen at least in our lifetimes, and with each proposal, the special interests come up with reasons why we shouldn't do it."

Representative Robert E. Andrews, Democrat of New Jersey, who has introduced legislation in the House to create national ballistic fingerprinting, said, "The technology is not perfect, but it's helpful."

Killings May Not Affect Gun Control Measures

BY KATHARINE Q. SEELYE | OCT. 20, 2002

AFTER THREE WEEKS of silence as a sniper stalked the Washington suburbs, the head of the gun lobby today dismissed talk of a ballistic fingerprinting system as a "technical fantasy" and predicted that Congress would enact no new legislation in response to the killings.

Wayne LaPierre, executive director of the National Rifle Association, said in an interview that he did not expect the sniper to alter the politics of gun control.

"With every tragedy that involves firearms, whether it's a post office shooting or a school shooting, you have an opportunistic attempt by gun control groups and some politicians to never miss a chance to trade on a tragedy and politicize the debate," Mr. LaPierre said. "But they're trying to ride the same old tired horse. There's nothing new in what they're proposing, and it's not resonating."

Even gun control advocates do not expect any legislation to be enacted in response to the sniper, and few have much hope that they will prevail on the next milestone in the gun debate, which is to strengthen the ban on assault weapons when it comes up for renewal in September 2004.

Asked if the sniper killings had reinvigorated the gun control movement, Senator Charles E. Schumer, the New York Democrat who made his name in 1994 advancing the ban on assault weapons, said, "With a pro-gun president in the White House and one house of Congress in Republican hands and the other so narrowly divided, it's an uphill fight."

There are exceptions to this conventional wisdom. The House Republican leadership last week called off a vote on a bill that would have granted the gun industry sweeping immunity from lawsuits. The bill was a big priority for the rifle association, which has engineered such legislation in 30 states.

Federal officials investigate after a shooting in Manassas, Va., on Oct. 10, 2002, that was linked to the DC-area sniper attacks.

In Maryland, where 6 of the 11 sniper victims were killed, the issue of gun control has come into stark relief. It is part of the dialogue in the governor's race between Kathleen Kennedy Townsend, the Democrat, whose father, Robert F. Kennedy, was shot to death, and Robert Ehrlich, the Republican, who has generally opposed gun control.

In Pennsylvania, Edward G. Rendell, the former Philadelphia mayor and now a Democratic candidate for governor, has not flinched in his opposition to the gun lobby and appears likely to win on Election Day.

The sniper has also revived interest among gun control advocates in a national database of ballistics "fingerprints," the electronic images of the unique markings that every gun makes on the bullet it fires.

But the rifle group is adamantly opposed to such a database, saying it is unproven, would be burdensome and would lead to their worst nightmare — a national gun registry.

Gun control forces admit privately that such a plan has scant chance of moving through Congress, and there is little sign that the debate in Maryland has taken hold elsewhere.

National Rifle Association officials are still planning a campaign swing next week with Charlton Heston, the group's president, on behalf of their candidates in competitive Senate and gubernatorial races.

Mr. LaPierre said that since the shootings began, none of the candidates endorsed by the rifle association had tried to distance themselves from the gun lobby. "You still have candidates, even Democrats, with shotguns, getting their pictures taken at the shooting range," he said.

Senator Trent Lott, Republican of Mississippi, shrugged off any suggestion that the sniper might alter the political debate.

"I know that in the West and the South, we like — we feel like we have the right to bear arms, and we have them, we have lots of them," Senator Lott told reporters. "And we generally don't shoot our neighbors with them, either."

Mathew S. Nosanchuk, litigation director of the Violence Policy Center, a gun control research group based in Washington, conceded, "There is not a lot of momentum."

By contrast, after the 1999 massacre by two students at Columbine High School in Colorado, the Clinton administration led a crusade joined by many in Congress for renewed gun control measures. These included closing a gun-show loophole, requiring mandatory trigger locks on all new handguns, raising the age for buying guns to 21 from 18 and banning the import of high-capacity ammunition clips.

But even with the momentum spurred by Columbine, none of these measures were enacted.

Now with the sniper, any outcry for legislative action is more limited and the prospects are just as dim. For one thing, the Bush administration opposes gun control. Members of Congress, at least half of whom oppose gun control, have left town. Also, the sniper has not been caught. That means no one yet knows the circumstances under which he obtained his weapon or weapons, and the focus is still on catching him.

The House did pass legislation last week by voice vote to provide more money to enhance background checks, a measure that is expected to clear the Senate, too. But this was not as contentious an issue as the national ballistics database.

The White House initially came out against the database, with Ari Fleischer, the spokesman, saying that it did not work. He later said it should be studied.

Mr. LaPierre said he thought that perhaps the White House realized that the public needed to be "educated" about ballistics fingerprinting before it would accept President Bush's position.

Michael D. Barnes, president of the Brady Campaign to Prevent Gun Violence, said of Mr. Fleischer's reformulated response, "The political people at the White House must have gasped and realized that it was a very unfortunate thing to say when people are dying that we're not going to use every tool available to try to catch the guy."

While no one suggests that President Bush would support ballistics fingerprinting, Mr. Barnes said he believed that the White House had a keen understanding of the importance of gun control to suburban Republican women.

"Republicans know they can't win statewide in swing states like Pennsylvania and Michigan and Illinois and New Jersey if they're on the wrong side of the gun issue," Mr. Barnes said.

Democrats are more subdued these days about pushing the issue. Senator Schumer, for example, proselytized for the assault-weapons ban in 1994, but now says that the most he hopes for is meeting the Second Amendment advocates halfway on law enforcement and dropping talk of gun control.

"The loss of the gun-show loophole after Columbine discouraged people," he said. "Before, we would have said 'Ban the gun.' Now we say, 'Let's have a system where law enforcement can find the criminal.' "

At the same time, the gun lobby seems to have evolved into a more politically sophisticated operation.

"The vehemence of the anti-gun-control lobby is not as strong," Mr. Schumer said. "They've seen some laws go on the books and it hasn't hurt them."

In the old days, their strong language, intended to rally the faithful, alienated the mainstream. For example, in a 1995 fund-raising letter, Mr. LaPierre said the assault weapon ban gave "jackbooted government thugs more power to take away our constitutional rights," prompting former President George Bush to quit the N.R.A. in protest.

Once the sniper attacks began, Mr. LaPierre fell silent, refusing all requests for comment until now. Had he learned a lesson that his language sometimes inflamed the other side?

No, he replied, saying his past remarks had been taken out of context. In this case, Mr. LaPierre said, not speaking out while the killer is still on the loose is just being responsible.

"I believe with all my heart we're the good guys," Mr. LaPierre said. "There are N.R.A. members out there right now, putting their lives on the line trying to catch this guy. It may be one of our members who catches this guy."

Vital Statistics

OPINION | BY BOB HERBERT | OCT. 31, 2002

JOHN MUHAMMAD and Lee Malvo are accused of killing 10 people during their terrifying three-week sniping spree in and around Washington.

On Monday a student at the University of Arizona carried five handguns and a couple of hundred rounds of ammunition into a nursing school and proceeded to kill three of his teachers and himself.

In Nashville, federal authorities announced this week that they will seek the death penalty against three drug traffickers accused of murdering seven people and seriously wounding a 3-year-old girl. In New York City, a man is on trial for the execution-style murder of five people in a Wendy's restaurant. An alleged accomplice has already pleaded guilty.

What these hideous cases all have in common, apart from the grief and suffering endured by the victims and their survivors, is that statistically none of them are that big a deal. Ten people here, five people there — very small potatoes in the crucible of criminal violence that we've got going here in the United States. Even the total number of people killed in the terrorist attacks of Sept. 11, 2001 — approximately 3,000 — is dwarfed by the annual toll of homicides in the U.S.

The F.B.I.'s annual Uniform Crime Report was released Monday. It showed that in 2001, the last year for which complete statistics have been compiled, the number of people murdered in the U.S. — exclusive of the Sept. 11 attacks — was a staggering 15,980.

There were no screaming headlines to accompany this disclosure because more than 15,000 people are murdered in the U.S. every year, most of them by firearms.

It might be a good idea to pay more attention to this.

In the spring of 1999, more than three years before the siege of sniper shootings in the Washington area, the Violence Policy Center, a gun control advocacy group, issued a warning about "the dangers posed by the civilian sale of military sniper rifles."

The center's report documented the gun industry's efforts "to market sniper rifles and the resulting subculture of sniper enthusiasts that have turned discussion of this weapon into a cottage industry of books, Web sites, computer games and even sniper schools."

Mr. Muhammad and Mr. Malvo are now in custody, but the deadly threat of sniper rifles and the sniper subculture remains. And not much is being done about it.

Despite the terrible toll that guns in the wrong hands are taking, there is tremendous resistance to even the most modest efforts to control the spread of guns among criminals. That resistance is led, as usual, by the National Rifle Association, which can always be counted on to provide a comfort zone for the perpetrators of gun violence in America.

The N.R.A. is opposed, for example, to the creation of a national computerized system for tracing bullets and shell casings to the guns that fired them — a crime-fighting tool that has come to be known as "ballistic fingerprinting."

Senators Charles Schumer of New York and Herb Kohl of Wisconsin have introduced legislation that would establish such a system, and it has the strong backing of Americans for Gun Safety, which describes itself as a centrist organization that believes in the rights of law-abiding citizens to own guns. But, so far, the proposal has gone nowhere.

Senator Schumer told me yesterday that if the investigators in the sniper shooting had been able to use this technology to trace the murder weapon at the start of the killing spree, the case could have been solved weeks earlier, and lives would have been saved.

Another modest attempt to thwart the sale of guns to criminals has been the effort to close a loophole in the Brady law that allows unlicensed individuals to sell firearms at gun shows without conducting background checks on the buyers.

Illegal gun traffickers flock to these shows, which account for the sale of hundreds of thousands of guns each year. "The criminals have figured it out," said Matt Bennett, a spokesman for Americans for Gun Safety. "They know that for the most part they can't just walk into an honest gun store anymore and buy a gun, so they go to the shows, where there is a huge variety and enormous volume."

Close the loophole and save lives? Move toward ballistic finger-printing? They sound like good ideas. But the U.S., with more than 15,000 homicide victims a year, can't get it done.

Millennial Changes in Gun Legislation

The early 2000s brought many setbacks to gun control advocates. The N.R.A. saw increased lobbying power throughout much of the decade. In 2004, Congress allowed the ban on assault rifles, called the Violent Crime Control and Law Enforcement Act of 1994, to expire. That same year Congress failed to gain enough funding to implement President George W. Bush's 2001 gun control program, called Project Safe Neighborhoods. The next year, President Bush signed the Protection of Lawful Commerce in Arms Act, which limited the ability of victims to sue firearms manufacturers or dealers for injuries caused by their guns.

More Guns for Everyone!

OPINION | BY BOB HERBERT | MAY 9, 2002

LET'S SEE. What America needs is more guns in the hands of more people, right?

That would almost certainly be the result of a new and potentially tragic initiative by John Ashcroft's Justice Department. In a reversal of federal policy that has stood for more than 60 years, the department told the Supreme Court this week that individual Americans have a constitutional right to own guns.

That sound you hear is the National Rifle Association cheering.

The N.R.A. has seldom had a better friend in government than Mr. Ashcroft. That was proved again on Monday when the Justice

Department, in a pair of briefs filed with the court, rejected the long-held view of the court, the Justice Department itself and most legal scholars that the Second Amendment protects only the right of state-organized militias to own firearms. Under that interpretation, anchored by a Supreme Court ruling in 1939, Congress and local governmental authorities have great freedom to regulate the possession and use of firearms by individuals.

In the briefs, submitted by Solicitor General Theodore Olson, the department boldly and gratuitously asserted, "The current position of the United States, however, is that the Second Amendment more broadly protects the right of individuals, including persons who are not members of any militia or engaged in active military service or training, to possess and bear their own firearms, subject to reasonable restrictions designed to prevent possession by unfit persons or to restrict the possession of types of firearms that are particularly suited to criminal misuse."

The move was gratuitous because there was no need for the government to take a position on the Second Amendment in the two cases for which the briefs were submitted. In both cases the Justice Department is defending gun laws. In one case it agrees that a man under a restraining order because of domestic violence should not be allowed to have a gun, and in the other it is opposing the appeal of a man convicted of illegally possessing machine guns.

The reference in the briefs to restrictions on "firearms that are particularly suited to criminal misuse" is interesting, and disingenuous. No gun is more suited to criminal misuse than a handgun, and that's exactly the type of weapon that Mr. Ashcroft and his N.R.A. pals are trying to make available to more and more American men and women.

I had a .45-caliber pistol hanging low on my hip many years ago when I was in the Army. And I can tell you, I'm not anxious to think about that kind of weapon (or something smaller and easier to conceal) being in the pockets and the purses and the briefcases and the shoulder holsters of the throngs surrounding me in my daily rounds in Manhattan.

How weird is it that in this post-Sept.-11 atmosphere, when the Justice Department itself is in the forefront of the effort to narrow potential threats to security, the attorney general decides it would be a good idea to throw open the doors to a wholesale increase in gun ownership?

Mr. Ashcroft telegraphed this transparently political move nearly a year ago in a letter to the N.R.A, which just happened to have been a major Ashcroft campaign contributor. The letter went from Mr. Ashcroft, who was already the attorney general, to the N.R.A.'s chief lobbyist, James J. Baker. Mr. Ashcroft wrote, "Let me state unequivocally my view that the text and the original intent of the Second Amendment clearly protect the right of individuals to keep and bear firearms. While some have argued that the Second Amendment guarantees only a 'collective right' of the states to maintain militias, I believe the amendment's plain meaning and original intent prove otherwise."

Now that view is the policy of the Bush administration. It will encourage aficionados and accused criminals to challenge gun control laws on constitutional grounds.

"Now defendants are going to try to make this Second Amendment argument, relying in part on Ashcroft's position," said Mathew Nosanchuk, the litigation director for the Violence Policy Center, a Washington group that advocates gun control.

The center has pointed out that in 1999, the most recent year for which statistics are available, 28,874 Americans were killed with guns.

Neither Mr. Ashcroft nor the N.R.A. seems particularly concerned.

Rethinking Ballistic Fingerprints

EDITORIAL | BY THE NEW YORK TIMES | NOV. 11, 2002

FORENSIC SCIENTISTS are all the rage on television these days. In real life, too, ballistics experts have become crime-fighting stars in the Beltway sniper case, where they linked most of the bullets to a single gun — the rifle later seized from John Muhammad — through their distinctive markings. But the frustrations encountered in trying to find the sniper have sparked calls, by this page among others, for a computerized national database of bullet and cartridge-case markings for all guns sold in the United States. Such a tool could help police track down a criminal more quickly.

The potential for solving crimes through such databases seems breathtaking. But another look at the science involved has convinced us that first, the government must get an authoritative judgment on how feasible the project really is. There is no point in setting up a system that might fail.

Right now, the nation has a network of smaller databases that are limited to evidence gathered by police in criminal investigations. That includes the bullets and cartridge cases found at crime scenes and those fired in tests of guns seized from criminals. This system has already helped solve a number of crimes and has wide support on all sides of the gun control debate.

The big question now is whether the nation should scale up this system to include the markings made by virtually all new handguns and rifles. Manufacturers could test fire the guns before shipping them to dealers, and submit the bullets and shell casings for inclusion in the database. Later, when a bullet or cartridge case is recovered from a crime scene, its markings could be compared with those in the database. If a match was found, police would know what gun was responsible and could try to trace its ownership.

The gun lobbies have adamantly opposed such a system, mostly for reasons that seem unpersuasive, such as their fear that the database could turn into a national gun registry. They also claim the markings made by guns change with repeated firing, something that seems to be a problem only with lead bullets, not the more common jacketed ones or the cartridge cases. While it is true that criminals could alter a gun to change its markings, experts say that in real life lawbreakers rarely do this, just as they rarely wear gloves to hide their fingerprints.

The real obstacle confronting a large-scale system is whether the computer programs can find the proverbial needles in a very big haystack. The automated searches do not conclusively identify a culprit weapon; they simply try to narrow the field to a small number of suspect bullets or shell casings that can be examined under the microscope to clinch the identification. Many experts worry that the automated searches wouldn't be discriminating enough to work with a huge database. In tests carried out by the state of California, the automated searches had an alarming failure rate — as high as 62.5 percent.

Federal experts believe the California tests were flawed and say their own tests show much higher accuracy. That technical dispute needs careful evaluation. So does the issue of costs and practicality. Some examiners fear a large system might gobble up manpower and resources with little to show for it, whereas other enthusiasts believe that as the system grows it could become as valuable as existing fingerprint databases.

Gun control advocates worry that studying the issue will inevitably mean delaying the proposal to death. That need not be the case. The study could be given a short deadline and entrusted to a respected organization like the National Academy of Sciences. The benefits of a successful system would be immense, but the backlash from a large, messy failure would be a terrible setback for the entire effort to control the misuse of firearms.

Democrats, Using Finesse, Try to Neutralize the Gun Lobby's Muscle

BY KATHARINE Q. SEELYE | SEPT. 10, 2002

SENATOR JEAN CARNAHAN, the Missouri Democrat, pulled out her 20-gauge Browning Citori shotgun the other day and fired off a few rounds as part of a skeet-shoot benefit for a home state research center.

In Alaska, Lt. Gov. Fran Ulmer, the Democratic candidate for governor and owner of a permit to carry a concealed weapon, went gun shopping in July with reporters in tow. Ms. Ulmer, who owns eight firearms, mostly rifles, told The Anchorage Daily News that she needed something to make her feel safe on the campaign trail — and that she did not own anything small enough to fit in her purse.

In New Mexico, Bill Richardson, the Democratic candidate for governor, was a member of the Clinton cabinet and former ambassador to the United Nations. Although his voting record in Congress was generally pro-gun, his association with the antigun Clinton administration is enough to worry the gun lobby. Anticipating such concern, Mr. Richardson is marketing himself as "the choice for New Mexico gun owners and sportsmen."

These Democrats and others nationwide are well aware that gun owners cost Al Gore crucial votes in a handful of states in the 2000 presidential election, including Tennessee, his home state. They are also aware that Mark Warner, a Democrat who was elected governor of Virginia in 2001, neutralized the gun issue in his campaign by reassuring white male voters in rural areas that he did not want to take their guns.

As a result, many candidates this year are eagerly emulating the Warner model. Across the country and across party lines, candidates — many of whom are running on a big day of primaries on Tuesday — are supplicants to their pro-gun-rights constituents. They may not be advancing the agenda of the National Rifle Association, but they do not want to alienate the powerful gun lobby.

Rather, they are trying to inoculate themselves against the N.R.A.'s Election Day forces.

The association endured organizational problems in the 1990's but has since rebuilt its fund-raising and remains an important force in the Republican Party.

Now, Democrats are so eager for the gun lobby's endorsement that the rifle association is involved in three times as many Democratic primaries this year as it was during the 2000 elections, said Andrew Arulanandam, a spokesman for the association.

Gun control advocates concede that some candidates need to assuage their constituents who own guns. But, they argue, that does not reflect the sentiment in most of the country.

"There is no question that candidates running in rural areas — Democrats and Republicans — find themselves forced to cater to the gun lobby," said Michael Barnes, a former Democratic representative from Maryland and now president of the Brady Campaign to Prevent Gun Violence, formerly Handgun Control. "And you've got such a pro-gun administration — Bush, Cheney, Ashcroft are all so extreme on the issue — that there's more focus on it."

But, Mr. Barnes cautioned, "the N.R.A. is running against the tide of demography in the United States."

Wayne LaPierre, executive vice president of the National Rifle Association, countered: "There's been a sea change on this issue since the 2000 election. Democrats are running away from gun control like the plague, and we are just not being attacked. If they're not agreeing with us, they're silent. They're either looking for the N.R.A. endorsement or they're making sure the N.R.A. doesn't do anything against them."

The rifle association will not endorse candidates until late October. But it is leaning toward giving its blessing to more Democrats than ever before.

"Because more Democrats are restructuring their position, that may happen," Mr. Arulanandam said. "But our endorsement process is fairly rigid. We're concerned that we might have a lot of fair-weather friends. These people are obviously paying attention to the changing political winds and right now everyone is currying favor with the N.R.A., but will they be there when something bad happens and we need their vote?"

Mr. Barnes said Democrats for gun control needed to hold their ground.

"Democratic members of Congress might be saying the party has to focus on rural white males, but my response to that is, if you believe the future of American politics is winning the votes of rural white males, you're crazy," he said. "The future is the suburbs, especially women."

The affluent suburbs of big cities are still among the most reliably antigun strongholds in the country. In suburban Maryland, all five candidates — four Democrats and the Republican incumbent — for the House support gun control. Mark K. Shriver and Christopher Van Hollen Jr., both Democrats, are each running television commercials declaiming their antigun credentials; the winner of their Sept. 10 primary will face Representative Constance A. Morella, a Republican who is already advertising the fact that she has been endorsed by the Brady Campaign.

Such jousting in the suburbs, however, seems to be the exception.

Not far from Ms. Morella's suburban Maryland district is a rural House district where Representative Wayne T. Gilchrest, a six-term moderate Republican, is being challenged by a conservative Republican in the Sept. 10 primary. Mr. Gilchrest is running commercials calling himself a "Marine hero, longtime N.R.A. member who understands the need to protect our Second Amendment rights." (Officials from the gun lobby say Mr. Gilchrest joined their organization only in June.)

In Tennessee, where Mr. Gore lost in 2000 to George W. Bush by 47 percent to 51 percent, several Democratic candidates are similarly casting themselves as the sportsman's friend. These include Lincoln Davis, running for the House seat where Mr. Gore began his political career. He has the backing of the former vice president and the gun lobby.

Steve Rosenthal, political director of the A.F.L.-C.I.O., said that in 2000 the labor movement was "extremely antsy" about the gun issue because the gun lobby was making inroads with union members based on their cultural affiliation with guns.

"We had to say, 'It's not about guns; it's about your family's economic security,' " Mr. Rosenthal said. "And we'd say, 'Gore doesn't want to take away your gun, but Bush wants to take away your union.'

"In places where we took them head-on, we won," he said, adding that 58 percent of union members who own guns voted for Mr. Gore, while 37 percent voted for Mr. Bush.

This year, Mr. Rosenthal said, "our folks are encouraging candidates to keep the spotlight off the gun issue."

This season, gun control has vanished from the Democrats' agenda on Capitol Hill. The Senate and the House have bills that would give gun makers federal immunity against civil lawsuits, but analysts predict there will not be any votes on major gun legislation before the election.

Gun Strategists Are Watching Brooklyn Case

BY WILLIAM GLABERSON | OCT. 5, 2002

A BROOKLYN LAWSUIT has become a pivotal test that could affect civil suits against the gun industry nationally because the plaintiffs have, for the first time, obtained comprehensive government information tracing gun sales.

The information given to the plaintiffs' lawyers in the Brooklyn case by the Bureau of Alcohol, Tobacco and Firearms includes the sales history of guns used in crimes. Critics of the gun industry have long sought the information to try to fill what some courts have said has been missing from their cases: evidence that manufacturers knew how their guns were channeled toward illegal uses and an indication that they could have stopped the trafficking.

From coast to coast, a contention of many of the nearly 30 suits against the gun industry is that some manufacturers' handguns are used in crimes so frequently that their sales strategies amount to a violation of the public's right to safety and peace.

Experts on liability law and the firearms industry say the information tracing gun sales may give the plaintiffs their best chance at trying to prove what they say is a "hear no evil, see no evil" policy by gun makers toward the distribution of their products.

The information, gathered by the bureau when it traces guns at the request of law enforcement officials, shows the path of guns from manufacturers to specific wholesalers and retailers and then, in many instances, to shootings. "The trace data is the Rosetta stone of following gun crime," said Jim Kessler, policy director of Americans for Gun Safety, a group that supports gun rights and stronger laws to limit improper uses of firearms.

The federal government has long resisted release of the information, saying it could be harmful to each of more than one million criminal investigations reflected in the database. The Justice Department is now asking the United States Supreme Court to review a ruling in a Chicago case that would release the same information under the Freedom of Information Act.

On Sept. 27, after an agreement in United States District Court in Brooklyn, the government turned over the information to the National Association for the Advancement of Colored People, which filed a suit against the gun industry in 1999. In a court hearing yesterday, lawyers agreed to begin the trial in February or March.

Lawyers for the firearms bureau declined to comment on why they agreed to release the information. But lawyers involved in the case said the judge, Jack B. Weinstein, had indicated that he was likely to give the information to the plaintiffs as part of their discovery request. The bureau then made its unusual deal to provide the information, but insisted on a court order requiring that no identifying details be released, even during testimony in the case.

Lawyers for the gun industry said the data would not establish any liability because it could show only that manufacturers and their distributors sell a legal product through legal means. "What the plaintiffs are trying to do is bootstrap a case out of a misuse of data," said James P. Dorr, a Chicago lawyer who represents Sturm, Ruger & Company, one of the country's largest gun makers.

But as word spread of the agreement by the bureau to provide the information in recent days, many experts said the legal battle could be a watershed for the lawsuits against the gun industry.

Anthony J. Sebok, a professor at Brooklyn Law School who has written about the gun cases, said the new information could build a devastating case against the gun industry. But he also said that if the plaintiffs fail in the Brooklyn case, that could be a setback for all the lawsuits across the country. "It could end the campaign to use litigation as a method of achieving gun control," he said.

Elisa Barnes, the chief lawyer for the N.A.A.C.P. in the Brooklyn case, said the 11 years of gun-sales data she obtained from the federal government is being analyzed by experts on marketing, the gun industry and statistics who are working with her on the case. In filing the suit in 1999, the N.A.A.C.P. said its goal was "to protect the well-being and security of its membership, which has been disproportionately injured" by illegal handguns.

Some incomplete and dated information from the firearms agency has been available in the past, but Ms. Barnes said she expected the most useful material will be from newly released gun-tracing records from 1996 to 2000. Critics of the gun industry say it may be a gold mine, because more and more thorough investigations of gun sales are believed to have taken place during that period than ever.

Ms. Barnes acknowledged that the turn in her case presented a test for the strategy of taking on the gun industry in court. "I think it is the one important moment in this type of litigation," she said.

Ms. Barnes was the chief lawyer in the only case against the gun industry as a whole that ended with a verdict for the plaintiffs. That case, also before Judge Weinstein, ended in February 1999, with a finding that nine gun manufacturers were liable for shootings in the New York City region. That verdict was overturned in an unusual appeal that went to New York State's highest court, the Court of Appeals, because the federal court was interpreting state personal-injury law.

In its opinion, that court said Ms. Barnes's 1999 case failed, but some lawyers said the decision left the door open to another case with more solid evidence connecting the gun industry to the distribution of guns used in crimes. Liability, the court said, "should not be imposed without a more tangible showing that defendants were a direct link in the causal chain."

Ms. Barnes said the new case will provide that tangible evidence. But lawyers for the 165 gun makers and distributors named as defendants have said that her arguments are flawed. Timothy A. Bumann, a lawyer for a half dozen of the companies, said one weak point is Ms. Barnes's claim that the firearms bureau's data will prove that manufacturers whose guns regularly end up in illegal uses had a reason to know how that occurs.

Mr. Bumann said the fact that the bureau keeps its information confidential would undercut any argument Ms. Barnes makes to the jury. "If it's never seen the light of day before," he said, "how are the defendants supposed to have reacted to it?"

Critics of the gun industry have long argued that manufacturers know how many of their guns are traced by the bureau, because the bureau contacts the manufacturer to begin each trace.

Ms. Barnes made several strategic decisions that make the current case different from her 1999 case. Instead of seeking damages for the families of gun victims, for example, the current case seeks an injunction that would establish new restrictions on the marketing and distribution of handguns.

Although the trial is expected to include a great deal of evidence about statistical and marketing issues, Ms. Barnes said she would call some members of the N.A.A.C.P. who could testify about the legacy of gun violence. One of them is scheduled to be Gladys Gerena, whose 16-year-old son, Shaun, went to the store one day in Williamsburg, Brooklyn, to buy a sandwich and never came home. Neither the gun nor the man who shot him to death on Sept. 1, 1995, has been found.

In an interview, Ms. Gerena said she was taking part in the suit to try to establish some accountability. "I don't think anybody should make money from people dying," she said, "and they're dying because of these illegal guns on the street."

U.S. Appeals Court Upholds
Limits on Assault Weapons

BY ADAM LIPTAK | DEC. 2, 2002

THE FEDERAL APPEALS COURT in San Francisco yesterday unanimously upheld most aspects of a California law restricting sales and ownership of the semiautomatic firearms sometimes called assault weapons. It rejected a challenge to the law based on recent interpretations of the Second Amendment by a federal appeals court in New Orleans and by the Justice Department.

The law, enacted in 1989 and broadened in 1999, was challenged by people who owned or wanted to buy such firearms.

The decision is significant, legal experts said, not for its outcome, which was largely required by earlier decisions of the court, but for its extended rebuttal of more recent interpretations of the Second Amendment. The ruling was issued by the United States Court of Appeals for the Ninth Circuit.

In 2001, the United States Court of Appeals for the Fifth Circuit, in New Orleans, ruled that the Second Amendment broadly protected the rights of individuals to own guns. Yesterday's decision took the contrary view, holding that the amendment protects only a collective right to organize state militias.

Judge Stephen Reinhardt, writing for two members of a three-judge panel, said a rebuttal was warranted because, except for the 2001 decision, "there exists no thorough judicial examination of the amendment's meaning."

Judge Reinhardt described the Supreme Court's most extensive treatment of the question, in 1939, as "somewhat cryptic." Courts have generally interpreted that decision to support, though obliquely, the collective-rights model.

In footnotes in two filings with the Supreme Court in May, the Justice Department reversed a view it had espoused for decades and said the Second Amendment protected the rights of individuals "to possess and bear their own firearms, subject to reasonable restrictions."

Judge Reinhardt, generally considered to be one of the nation's most liberal jurists, concluded that the text and history of the Second Amendment and judicial decisions interpreting it all supported the view that the amendment protects only "the right of the people to maintain effective militias."

The panel struck down as irrational a provision of the law that allowed retired law enforcement officers to retain assault weapons.

Judge Raymond C. Fisher joined in the opinion. A visiting federal appeals court judge, Frank J. Magill, voted to uphold the law, but declined to join in the majority's discussion of the Second Amendment. In light of precedent in the Ninth Circuit, Judge Magill wrote, "it is unnecessary and improper to reach the merits of the Second Amendment claims or to explore the contour of the Second Amendment debate."

Revised View of 2nd Amendment Is Cited as Defense in Gun Cases

BY ADAM LIPTAK | JULY 23, 2003

SCORES OF CRIMINAL defendants around the nation have asked federal courts to dismiss gun charges against them based on the Justice Department's recently revised position on the scope of the Second Amendment.

The new position, that the Constitution broadly protects the rights of individuals to own guns, replaced the view, endorsed by the great majority of courts, that the amendment protects a collective right of the states to maintain militias.

While the challenges have been rejected by trial court judges, based largely on appeals court precedent, supporters and opponents of broad antigun laws say the arguments have forced the Justice Department to take contradictory stances.

Andrew L. Frey, a deputy solicitor general in the Justice Department from 1973 to 1986, said the department's new position would make life difficult for prosecutors and might give criminal defendants unforeseen opportunities.

"Is this a Pandora's box, which, when once opened, cannot be controlled?" asked Mr. Frey, who opposed the new position in a letter to Justice Department officials on behalf of a gun-control group.

A spokeswoman for the Justice Department, Monica Goodling, said the department was committed to prosecuting gun crimes.

"The department believes it can defend the constitutionality of all existing federal firearms laws while working to take guns out of the hands of those who abuse them," Ms. Goodling said.

In briefs filed with the Supreme Court in May, department lawyers said laws that restrict gun ownership by unfit people or restrict ownership of guns "particularly suited for criminal misuse" are appropriate.

The department faces the clearest contradictions of its stance in Washington, which has an essentially complete ban on handguns. The city's government is supervised by Congress, and its local crimes are prosecuted by the Justice Department.

Ms. Goodling was more guarded in discussing the District of Columbia's gun law.

"The department can defend its criminal prosecutions of the firearms laws in D.C., and is doing so," she said. The difference in wording suggests that the department is unwilling to endorse the constitutionality of Washington's gun law in all circumstances.

People on both sides of the gun control debate find fault with the department.

"The Justice Department has created a very dangerous situation that is endangering public safety and forcing Justice Department prosecutors to litigate with one hand tied behind their backs," said Mathew S. Nosanchuk, litigation director of the Violence Policy Center, a gun control group in Washington. "Criminals are using the department's own Second Amendment language to challenge the gun laws."

On the other hand, Robert A. Levy of the Cato Institute, a libertarian research group in Washington, was critical of Attorney General John Ashcroft for announcing the new position in briefs to the Supreme Court in May but not applying it in trial courts.

"It's bizarre for Ashcroft to go out of his way to assert that the Second Amendment is about an individual right when he didn't have to say anything," Mr. Levy said. "When he has the chance to make the assertion in a case where it really matters, he doesn't. It's puzzling."

Prosecutors opposing the new Second Amendment challenges have filed narrow and cryptic responses. In a brief filed in the District of Columbia Court of Appeals, for instance, the Justice Department noted that its position on the Second Amendment was inconsistent with that of the court, which has held that the amendment protects a collective right. Still, it continued, "although the question of the proper interpretation of the Second Amendment is significant, this case simply does not present that question in a manner suitable for resolution."

In other briefs, the government has argued that a particular defendant or weapon fits within its own announced exceptions. According to a brief filed in San Francisco, "The government does not concede that the Second Amendment creates a fundamental individual right for felons to bear arms, or for anyone to bear arms" like the machine guns at issue in that case.

The Supreme Court last addressed the meaning of the Second Amendment in 1939, in a decision that lawyers on both sides of the issue say supports their views. That disagreement about Supreme Court precedent, along with a federal appeals court decision last year adopting the individual-rights view, means it is an open question how other appeals courts will view the new challenges.

In footnotes in two filings with the Supreme Court in May, the government said the Second Amendment protected the rights of individuals "to possess and bear their own firearms, subject to reasonable restrictions designed to prevent possession by unfit persons or to restrict the possessions of types of firearms that are particularly suited to criminal misuse."

Defendants have said this position amounts to a recognition that the right to bear arms is as fundamental as the right to free speech and so requires courts to be extremely skeptical of government efforts to regulate guns. That is a position that has long been held by groups opposing gun control.

Public defenders say they are engaged in a cat-and-mouse game with the government, with the goal of forcing it to articulate its true position.

The government's court filings, said John Paul Reichmuth, a federal public defender in Oakland, Calif., are "evasive and anemic to the point of unconsciousness." But, Mr. Reichmuth said, "at some point in some argument where a real case is going on, they won't be able to fall back on their procedural arguments and they'll have to state what the content of the right is."

An appeal in the most challenging case, that of the District of Columbia's gun law, has already reached the local appellate court, the District of Columbia Court of Appeals. It was filed by Bashuan Pearson, who was charged with felony weapons possession. In court papers, Mr. Pearson said that he had a license to carry the pistol in question in Maryland and that he had a clean criminal record.

Mr. Pearson complained to the appeals court that in its own court papers the Justice Department "refuses to reveal whether, under the current view of the attorney general concerning the meaning of the Second Amendment, the District's gun laws are facially unconstitutional."

Mr. Pearson asked for a full-court hearing. Only the full court can overrule an earlier precedent of the court, which held that the Second Amendment protects a collective right.

Apparently not satisfied that the Justice Department will adequately defend the local law, the District of Columbia's lawyers have asked to intervene in the case.

James C. McKay Jr., a lawyer for Washington, said Justice Department prosecutors must reconcile their day-to-day prosecutorial practices with the department's new policy. "There is a conflict between their very hard approach to gun possession and their position that there is a Second Amendment right to carry a gun," Mr. McKay said.

The government is allowed to take contrary legal positions in different settings, legal experts said. "The argument that you're being hypocritical is not a legally sufficient argument," said Akhil Reed Amar, a law professor at Yale.

But there are practical difficulties in reconciling warring positions in related litigations, said Michael Dorf, a law professor at Columbia.

"Ashcroft is trying to please two different constituencies," Mr. Dorf said. "On the one hand, there is the gun lobby, which is very pleased with his decision. On the other hand, he has to consider federal prose-cutors and probably the general public as well."

Mr. Frey, the former deputy solicitor general, said he hoped the question would remain academic.

"I hope the upshot will be that the attorney general's new position will be rejected and recede into the mists of history," he said, "or that it will turn out to be contentless in that there will be no cases to which it will apply."

Justices, Ruling 5-4, Endorse Personal Right to Own Gun

BY LINDA GREENHOUSE | JUNE 27, 2008

WASHINGTON — The Supreme Court on Thursday embraced the long-disputed view that the Second Amendment protects an individual right to own a gun for personal use, ruling 5 to 4 that there is a constitutional right to keep a loaded handgun at home for self-defense.

The landmark ruling overturned the District of Columbia ban on handguns, the strictest gun-control law in the country, and appeared certain to usher in a new round of litigation over gun rights throughout the country.

The court rejected the view that the Second Amendment's "right of the people to keep and bear arms" applied to gun ownership only in connection with service in the "well regulated militia" to which the amendment refers.

Justice Antonin Scalia's majority opinion, his most important in his 22 years on the court, said that the justices were "aware of the problem of handgun violence in this country" and "take seriously" the arguments in favor of prohibiting handgun ownership.

"But the enshrinement of constitutional rights necessarily takes certain policy choices off the table," he said, adding, "It is not the role of this court to pronounce the Second Amendment extinct."

Justice Scalia's opinion was signed by Chief Justice John G. Roberts Jr. and Justices Anthony M. Kennedy, Clarence Thomas and Samuel A. Alito Jr.

In a dissenting opinion, Justice John Paul Stevens took vigorous issue with Justice Scalia's assertion that it was the Second Amendment that had enshrined the individual right to own a gun. Rather, it was "today's law-changing decision" that bestowed the right and created "a dramatic upheaval in the law," Justice Stevens said in a dissent joined by Justices David H. Souter, Ruth Bader Ginsburg and Stephen

G. Breyer. Justice Breyer, also speaking for the others, filed a separate dissent.

Justice Scalia and Justice Stevens went head to head in debating how the 27 words in the Second Amendment should be interpreted. The majority opinion and two dissents ran 154 pages.

Justice Stevens said the majority opinion was based on "a strained and unpersuasive reading" of the text and history of the Second Amendment, which provides: "A well regulated militia, being necessary to the security of a free state, the right of the people to keep and bear arms, shall not be infringed."

According to Justice Scalia, the "militia" reference in the first part of the amendment simply "announces the purpose for which the right was codified: to prevent elimination of the militia." The Constitution's framers were afraid that the new federal government would disarm the populace, as the British had tried to do, Justice Scalia said.

But he added that this "prefatory statement of purpose" should not be interpreted to limit the meaning of what is called the operative clause — "the right of the people to keep and bear arms, shall not be infringed." Instead, Justice Scalia said, the operative clause "codified a pre-existing right" of individual gun ownership for private use.

Contesting that analysis, Justice Stevens said the Second Amendment's structure was notable for its "omission of any statement of purpose related to the right to use firearms for hunting or personal self-defense," in contrast to the contemporaneous "Declarations of Rights" in Pennsylvania and Vermont that did explicitly protect those uses.

It has been nearly 70 years since the court last examined the meaning of the Second Amendment. In addition to their linguistic debate, Justices Scalia and Stevens also sparred over what the court intended in that decision, United States v. Miller.

In the opaque, unanimous five-page opinion in 1939, the court upheld a federal prosecution for transporting a sawed-off shotgun. A Federal District Court had ruled that the provision of the National

Firearms Act the defendants were accused of violating was barred by the Second Amendment, but the Supreme Court disagreed and reinstated the indictment.

For decades, an overwhelming majority of courts and commentators regarded the Miller decision as having rejected the individual-right interpretation of the Second Amendment. That understanding of the "virtually unreasoned case" was mistaken, Justice Scalia said Thursday.

He said the Miller decision meant "only that the Second Amendment does not protect those weapons not typically possessed by law-abiding citizens for lawful purposes, such as short-barreled shotguns."

Justice Stevens said the majority's understanding of the Miller decision was not only "simply wrong," but also reflected a lack of "respect for the well-settled views of all of our predecessors on the court, and for the rule of law itself."

Despite the decision's enormous symbolic significance, it was far from clear that it actually posed much of a threat to the most common gun regulations. Justice Scalia's opinion applied explicitly just to "the right of law-abiding, responsible citizens to use arms in defense of hearth and home," and it had a number of significant qualifications.

"Nothing in our opinion," he said, "should be taken to cast doubt on longstanding prohibitions on the possession of firearms by felons and the mentally ill, or laws forbidding the carrying of firearms in sensitive places such as schools and government buildings, or laws imposing conditions and qualifications on the commercial sale of arms."

The opinion also said prohibitions on carrying concealed weapons would be upheld and suggested somewhat less explicitly that the right to personal possession did not apply to "dangerous and unusual weapons" that are not typically used for self-defense or recreation.

The Bush administration had been concerned about the implications of the case for the federal ban on possessing machine guns.

President Bush welcomed the decision. "As a longstanding advocate of the rights of gun owners in America," he said in a statement, "I applaud the Supreme Court's historic decision today confirming what has always been clear in the Constitution: the Second Amendment protects an individual right to keep and bear firearms."

The opinion did not specify the standard by which the court would evaluate gun restrictions in future cases, a question that was the subject of much debate when the case was argued in March.

Among existing gun-control laws, just Chicago comes close to the complete handgun prohibition in the District of Columbia's 32-year-old law. The district's appeal to the Supreme Court, filed last year after the federal appeals court here struck down the law, argued that the handgun ban was an important public safety measure in a congested, crime-ridden urban area.

On the campaign trail on Thursday, both major-party presidential candidates expressed support for the decision — more full-throated support from Senator John McCain, the presumptive Republican nominee, and a more guarded statement of support from Senator Barack Obama, his presumptive Democratic opponent.

Mr. McCain called the decision "a landmark victory for Second Amendment freedom in the United States" that "ended forever the specious argument that the Second Amendment did not confer an individual right to keep and bear arms."

Mr. Obama, who like Mr. McCain has been on record as supporting the individual-rights view, said the ruling would "provide much-needed guidance to local jurisdictions across the country."

He praised the decision for endorsing the individual-rights view and for describing the right as "not absolute and subject to reasonable regulations enacted by local communities to keep their streets safe."

Unlike the court's ruling this month on the rights of the Guantánamo detainees, this decision, District of Columbia v. Heller, No. 07-290, appeared likely to defuse, rather than inflame, the political debate. The Democratic Party platform in 2004 included a plank endorsing the individual-rights view of the Second Amendment.

The case reached the court as a result of an assumption by the Cato Institute, a libertarian organization here, that the time was right to test the prevailing interpretation of the Second Amendment. Robert A. Levy, a lawyer and senior fellow of the institute, looked for law-abiding district residents rather than criminal defendants appealing convictions, to challenge the law.

Mr. Levy, who financed the case, recruited six plaintiffs. Five were dismissed for lack of standing. But the United States Court of Appeals for the District of Columbia Circuit ruled in favor of one, Dick Anthony Heller. He is a security guard who carries a gun while on duty at a federal judicial building here and was denied a license to keep his gun at home. The court said Thursday that assuming Mr. Heller was not "disqualified from the exercise of Second Amendment rights," the district government must issue him a license.

Contemporary Calls to Action

In the wake of high-profile mass shootings from Connecticut (at Sandy Hook Elementary School in 2012) to Las Vegas (at a concert in 2017), there are more calls for gun control legislation than ever before. After a school shooting in Parkland, Fla., on Feb. 14, 2018, killed 17, polls showed that an increasing number of Americans support restrictions on guns, and several states passed stricter gun laws, such as banning assault weapons. Meanwhile, some gun advocates argue that schools would be safer if teachers were armed, demonstrating the sustained divide on gun control in the wake of these tragedies.

Nation's Pain Is Renewed, and Difficult Questions Are Asked Once More

BY WILLIAM GLABERSON | DEC. 14, 2012

ON FRIDAY, as Newtown, Conn., joined the list of places like Littleton, Colo., and Jonesboro, Ark., where schools became the scenes of stunning violence, the questions were familiar: Why does it happen? What can be done to stop it?

The questions have emerged after all of the mass killings in recent decades — at a Virginia college campus, a Colorado movie theater, a Wisconsin temple — but they took on an added sting when the victims included children.

The fact that the Newtown massacre, with 26 killed at the school, along with the gunman, was the second deadliest school shooting in the country's history — after the 32 people killed at Virginia Tech in 2007 — once again made this process of examination urgent national business as details emerged from Sandy Hook Elementary School.

This painful corner of modern American history does offer some answers: Many of the mass killers had histories of mental illness, with warning signs missed by the people who knew them and their sometimes clear signs of psychological deterioration left unaddressed by the country's mental health system.

The shootings almost always renew the debate about access to guns, and spur examination of security practices and missed warning signals in what were damaged lives.

Research on mass school killings shows that they are exceedingly rare. Amanda B. Nickerson, director of a center that studies school violence and abuse prevention at the University at Buffalo, said studies made clear that American schools were quite safe and that children were more likely to be killed outside of school.

But, she said, events like the Sandy Hook killings trigger fundamental fears. "When something like this happens," she said, "everybody says it's an epidemic, and that's just not true."

Dylan Klebold, 17, and Eric Harris, 18, may have earned singular infamy with the killing of 12 other students and a teacher from Columbine High School, in Littleton, Colo., in 1999, but there have been others who breached the safety of American schoolhouses over the decades.

In 1927, a school board official in Bath, Mich., killed 44 people, including students and teachers, when he blew up the town's school.

Even before Columbine in the late 1990s, school shootings seemed to be a national scourge, with killings in places like Jonesboro, Ark., and Springfield, Ore. In 2006, a 32-year-old man shot 11 girls at an Amish school in Nickel Mines, Pa., killing 5 of them.

Often in a haze of illness, the schoolhouse gunmen are usually aware of the taboo they are breaking by targeting children, said

Dewey G. Cornell, a clinical psychologist at the University of Virginia and director of the Virginia Youth Violence Project. "They know it's a tremendous statement that shocks people," Dr. Cornell said, "and that is a reflection of their tremendous pain and their drive to communicate that pain."

After 14-year-old Michael Carneal opened fire on a prayer group at Heath High School in West Paducah, Ky., in 1997, it came out that he had made no secret of his plans. "He told me, once or twice, that he thought it would be cool to walk — or run — down the halls shooting people," a friend from the school band testified later. Five Heath students were wounded; three were killed.

But some experts on school violence said Friday that it was not so much the character of the relatively rare schoolhouse gunman as it was the public perception of the shootings that transformed them into national and even international events. Dunblane, Scotland, is remembered for the day in 1996 when a 43-year-old man stormed a gym class of 5- and 6-year-olds, killing 16 children and a teacher.

Over the years there have been some indications of what warning signs to look for. The New York Times published an analysis in 2000 of what was known about 102 people who had committed 100 rampage killings at schools, job sites and public places like malls.

Most had left a road map of red flags, plotting their attacks and accumulating weapons. In the 100 rampage killings reviewed, 54 of the killers had talked explicitly of when and where they would act, and against whom. In 34 of the cases, worried friends or family members had desperately sought help in advance, only to be rebuffed by the police, school officials or mental health workers.

After the deaths in Sandy Hook on Friday, there was new talk of the need to be vigilant. But there has also been talk of the sober reality that it is hard to turn the ordinary places of life into fortresses.

Dr. Irwin Redlener, who is the director of the National Center for Disaster Preparedness at Columbia University and has worked on school violence issues, said there were steps that could be taken to try to limit school violence, like limiting entry, developing an explicit disaster plan that includes strategies to lock down schools and pursuing close ties with the local police.

"Unfortunately," he said, "random acts of severe violence like this are not possible to entirely prevent."

Obama Invokes Newtown Dead in Pressing for New Gun Laws

BY PETER APPLEBOME AND JONATHAN WEISMAN | APRIL 8, 2013

HARTFORD — President Obama came here on Monday before a roaring, enthusiastic crowd to remember the tragedy of 20 children and 6 educators slain at Sandy Hook Elementary School and put new pressure on a recalcitrant Congress to honor them with gun-control legislation.

In an impassioned speech that at times took on the tone of a campaign rally, Mr. Obama told an audience of 3,100 at the University of Hartford that he came to Connecticut to ensure that the deaths in the school in Newtown would not recede and to remind Americans how important their voice is as the gun debates unfold.

"If you're an American who wants to do something to prevent more families from knowing the immeasurable anguish that these families here have known, then we have to act," Mr. Obama said. "Now's the time to get engaged. Now's the time to get involved. Now's the time to push back on fear and frustration and misinformation. Now's the time for everybody to make their voices heard, from every statehouse to the corridors of Congress."

But as Mr. Obama spoke, Republicans on Capitol Hill were threatening to prevent a gun-control measure from even coming up for debate.

Senator Mitch McConnell of Kentucky, the Republican leader, announced Monday that he would join at least 13 other Republicans who have vowed to block consideration of gun legislation passed by the Senate Judiciary Committee and assembled by the Democratic leadership. That effectively made the threatened filibuster a test of Republican unity.

Mr. McConnell made his announcement as the Senate returned from recess and the legislative struggle over new gun safety legislation entered a critical phase. Senator Harry Reid of Nevada, the majority leader, took steps to force a vote to start a broad review of gun-control proposals and accused those threatening a filibuster of "blatant obstruction," even as they showed no signs of backing down.

"Shame on them," said Mr. Reid, a Democrat.

Mr. Obama spoke in Hartford less than a week after the Connecticut General Assembly passed a sweeping package of gun and mental health legislation with bipartisan support.

The president was introduced by Nicole Hockley, whose first-grade son, Dylan, was killed at Sandy Hook. She recalled her life with her two sons before the tragedy and said she no longer had the option of turning away from the effects of gun violence. She said she was convinced that she and others had approached Connecticut lawmakers with the "love and logic" that persuaded them to pass the bill. She believed that approach could work with Congress, she said.

"If you want to protect your children, if you want to avoid this loss, you will not turn away either," Ms. Hockley said. "Do something before our tragedy becomes your tragedy."

Mr. Obama, who last visited Connecticut for a raw and emotional memorial shortly after the Dec. 14 shootings in Newtown, met again with the victims' relatives before his speech. Afterward about a dozen family members left with him from Connecticut on Air Force One to make their case in Washington to members of Congress this week.

Mr. Obama, who was wearing a green Newtown bracelet, made reference in his speech to the brutal cases of recent mass violence from Aurora, Colo., to Virginia Tech. He pushed for a broad agenda that would include universal background checks for gun buyers, restraints on gun trafficking and a ban on assault weapons. But he focused on the background checks, which he said were supported by 90 percent of Americans. "There's only one thing that can stand in the way of change that just about everybody agrees on, and that's politics in Washington," he said.

Mr. Obama, who included remarks respectful of gun owners, said "common-sense" gun measures could be enacted that would acknowledge the rights of gun owners and the Second Amendment. But he said that at the very least, Newtown and similar tragedies demanded a vote in Congress on gun control issues.

"If our democracy's working the way it's supposed to and 90 percent of the American people agree on something, in the wake of a tragedy, you'd think this would not be a heavy lift," Mr. Obama said. "And yet some folks back in Washington are already floating the idea that they may use political stunts to prevent votes on any of these reforms. Think about that.

"They're not just saying they'll vote no on ideas that almost all Americans support," he said. "They're saying they'll do everything they can to even prevent any votes on these provisions. They're saying your opinion doesn't matter, and that's not right."

Still, Democrats said they were encouraged that senior Republicans, including Senators John McCain of Arizona and Lindsey Graham of South Carolina, had indicated that a filibuster of gun legislation would be a mistake.

Connecticut has enormous symbolism in almost every way in the gun debate. Beyond the tragedy, the state legislature last week passed a major package of new gun laws, joining states — including Colorado, Maryland and New York — that have moved to enact strong gun legislation as efforts have largely stalled in Washington. But bipartisan talks on Capitol Hill were continuing in an attempt to reach a compromise on background checks that could lead to a breakthrough.

The bills before Congress would make penalties for buying guns illegally more onerous, address trafficking, and greatly expand the number of sales covered by background checks, which gun control advocates see as an essential component. The fight over background checks has been about the balance between how far to expand the current checks at licensed dealers and conservatives' fears over a paper trail that they insist could lead to a de facto national gun registry.

Mr. Obama said, as he has in the past, that the day of the Newtown massacre was the toughest of his presidency. He said that a failure to respond on gun issues would be tough, too, but that he believed the nation was not as divided as its political culture could seem.

"We have to believe that every once in a while we set politics aside, and just do what's right," Mr. Obama said.

After the speech, as the Newtown family members boarded Air Force One, one mother wiped away tears and another held up a notebook. On it were written two words: "Love Wins."

When the president's plane landed at Joint Base Andrews near Washington, Mr. Obama could be seen through its windows gathered with the families. A White House official said he was telling them where matters stood in Congress ahead of their lobbying this week.

Then they exited together, the president standing at the portal as each passed to descend the Air Force One stairs. He returned to the White House by helicopter; they were driven in government vans to Washington.

PETER APPLEBOME reported from Hartford, and JONATHAN WEISMAN from Washington. JACKIE CALMES contributed reporting from Hartford, and JENNIFER STEINHAUER from Washington.

Want Gun Control?
Learn From the N.R.A.

OPINION | BY HAHRIE HAN | OCT. 4, 2017

IS HELPLESS OUTRAGE the only choice gun-control advocates have after Las Vegas? As the horrific news unfolded, share prices of major gun manufacturers rose. Market investors were trading on the ugly reality we all knew: Gun regulations would not change, but fear of them would drive sales.

Understanding the choices gun-control advocates have begins with understanding where the outsize power of the National Rifle Association originates.

Most people assume its power comes from money. The truth is that gun-control advocates have lots of money, too. Billionaires like Michael Bloomberg have pledged fortunes to supporting gun control. After mass shootings, support for sensible gun laws grows.

The N.R.A.'s power is not just about its money or number of supporters or a favorable political map. It has also built something that gun-control advocates lack: an organized base of grass-roots power.

I grew up in Texas and now live in California. I study grass-roots organizations. I am a gun-control advocate with childhood friends who are ardent gun-rights supporters. I have seen the different ways in which the gun-rights and gun-control movements have built their bases.

First, gun-control groups summon action among people who agree, while gun-rights groups engage people who do not necessarily agree in association with one another. Most people assume that people who join groups like the N.R.A. are people who support gun rights — but that is not always the case.

Consider the anti-abortion movement. The sociologist Ziad Munson has found that almost half of the activists on the front lines of the anti-abortion movement — those who protest outside abortion clinics —

Gun control advocates protesting outside the National Rifle Association's headquarters in Fairfax, Va., in 2015.

were not anti-abortion when they attended their first event. They attended because a friend asked them, they had just joined a new church, or they retired and had more free time. They stayed, however, because at these events, they found things we all want: friends, responsibility, a sense that what they are doing matters. By finding fellowship and responsibility, these people changed not only their views on abortion but also their commitment to act.

Local gun clubs and gun shops provide a similar structure for the gun-rights movement. There are more gun clubs and gun shops in the United States than there are McDonald's. (The proportion of gun clubs affiliated with the N.R.A. is notoriously hard to track.) My friends who support the N.R.A. did not join a club because of politics. They joined because they wanted somewhere to shoot their guns.

The base of the gun-control movement is defined not by clubs but by ideology: people who come to the movement and share a view on gun control and can be sent into action. The organizations then add up those actions to claim a base. We take it for granted that gun-control groups have to define their base by moral outrage. The truth is, it's a choice that movement leaders make. They can decide to work through structures or not.

Second, gun-control groups focus on persuasion, while gun-rights groups focus on identity. In many ways, my friends and I who disagree on guns are similar. But their views evolved after joining these gun groups. So did their identities. The gun-rights groups were not just persuading them to support gun rights; they were also helping my friends rearticulate their own lives in terms of a broader vision of the future. They were no longer just hunters. They were protectors of a way of life. That is why the N.R.A.'s version of gun rights is so intimately tied to questions of race and identity.

When I joined gun-control groups, I got messages about narrowly defined issues like background checks and safety locks. These messages were a pollster's dream, tested down to the comma to maximize the likelihood that I would donate or take action. But they never challenged me to rethink who I was or what my relationship to my community was.

Third, for gun-rights groups, the work of engaging with identity and getting people to associate rests on a choice leaders made to invest in building the capacity of ordinary people to participate — and lead — in politics. When I studied groups that were most effective at building a grass-roots base, I found that the key factor to success was the nature of the relationships they created. The most effective groups used relationships as a vehicle for bringing people off the sidelines of public life and teaching them to speak truth to power. You can't convince someone to rethink who they are or what responsibility they want to take for their community through a mailer.

I have two young children. After Sandy Hook, I joined several gun-control organizations in a desperate effort to do something. These organizations asked me for money and sent me links for places to send emails or make phone calls. But none introduced me to anyone else in the organization or invited me to strategize about what I could do. Instead, I felt like a prop in a game under their control. I eventually asked to be taken off their lists.

Many groups, like Everytown for Gun Safety, are doing vital work to build a movement in the face of the entrenched power of the N.R.A. Reform will take more than raising money or shifting public opinion. The currency that matters in grass-roots power is commitment.

Elected officials can recognize the difference between organizations that can activate only people who are in agreement and those that can transform people who are not. The N.R.A. got over 80,000 people from all over the country to attend its annual meeting in 2017. What gun-control organization can claim the same?

Building a movement will require organizations to invest in the leadership of ordinary people by equipping them with the motivations, skills and autonomy they need to act. Most organizations never give people that opportunity.

Since the 2016 election, we have seen people engaged and hungry for the opportunity to take meaningful action. The question is, will one of the deadliest shootings of Americans in United States history prompt gun-control leaders to give people that chance?

HAHRIE HAN is a professor of political science at the University of California, Santa Barbara, and the author of "How Organizations Develop Activists: Civic Associations and Leadership in the 21st Century."

Republicans Open to Banning 'Bump Stocks' Used in Massacre

BY SHERYL GAY STOLBERG AND TIFFANY HSU | OCT. 4, 2017

WASHINGTON — Top congressional Republicans, who have for decades resisted any legislative limits on guns, signaled on Wednesday that they would be open to banning the firearm accessory that the Las Vegas gunman used to transform his rifles to mimic automatic weapon fire.

For a generation, Republicans in Congress — often joined by conservative Democrats — have bottled up gun legislation, even as the carnage of mass shootings grew ever more gruesome and the weaponry ever more deadly. A decade ago, they blocked efforts to limit the size of magazines after the massacre at Virginia Tech. Five years later, Republican leaders thwarted bipartisan legislation to expand background checks of gun purchasers after the mass shooting at an elementary school in Newtown, Conn.

Last year, in the wake of the Orlando nightclub massacre, they blocked legislation to stop gun sales to buyers on terrorism watch lists.

But in this week's massacre in Las Vegas, lawmakers in both parties may have found the part of the weapons trade that few could countenance: previously obscure gun conversion kits, called "bump stocks," that turn semiautomatic weapons into weapons capable of firing in long, deadly bursts.

"I own a lot of guns, and as a hunter and sportsman, I think that's our right as Americans, but I don't understand the use of this bump stock," Senator John Cornyn of Texas, the No. 2 Republican in the Senate, said, adding, "It seems like it's an obvious area we ought to explore and see if it's something Congress needs to act on."

Mr. Cornyn said the continuing legality of the conversion kits was "a legitimate question," and told reporters he had asked Senator

Charles E. Grassley of Iowa, the Judiciary Committee chairman, to convene a hearing on that issue and any others that arise out of the Las Vegas investigation.

Other Republican senators, including Lindsey Graham of South Carolina, Orrin G. Hatch of Utah and Marco Rubio of Florida, said they would be open to considering legislation on bump stocks.

"We certainly want to learn more details on what occurred in Las Vegas," Mr. Rubio said, "and if there are vulnerabilities in federal law that we should be addressing to prevent such attacks in the future, we would always be open to that."

In the House, Representative Carlos Curbelo, Republican of Florida, said he was drafting bipartisan legislation banning the conversion kits. Representative Mark Meadows, the head of the conservative Freedom Caucus, also said he would be open to considering a bill, while Representative Bill Flores, Republican of Texas, called for an outright ban.

AL DRAGO FOR THE NEW YORK TIMES

Senators John Cornyn, left, and Lindsey Graham, both Republicans, said they would consider supporting a ban on so-called bump stocks.

"I think they should be banned," Mr. Flores told the newspaper The Hill. "There's no reason for a typical gun owner to own anything that converts a semiautomatic to something that behaves like an automatic."

In an often deadlocked Washington, none of the pronouncements guaranteed action. The National Rifle Association, which has poured tens of millions of dollars into Republican campaign coffers, remained mum on the bump stock discussion and could stop it cold.

And Erich Pratt, executive director of another gun rights group, Gun Owners of America, vowed to block any legislation.

"We see this as an item that is certainly protected by the Second Amendment, and realistically, they are already on the market, so passing a law banning them isn't going to stop bad guys like this creep in Las Vegas," he said.

But Senator Dianne Feinstein, the California Democrat, tried to force the issue, introducing legislation, backed by about two dozen Democrats, that would ban bump stocks.

Ms. Feinstein cautioned that bipartisan support for such narrow legislation would hardly constitute a sea change. She tried to ban bump stocks in 2013, but that was part of broader legislation to renew the assault weapons ban, which went nowhere.

"I mean, if not this, what?" she asked. "It doesn't take a weapon away. It just means you can't convert it into something it's not meant to be."

At a hastily convened news conference, Ms. Feinstein said the Las Vegas massacre, which left 58 people dead and about 500 injured at a country music festival Sunday night, had hit home with her. Her daughter had planned to attend the concert but decided against going at the last minute.

Ms. Feinstein, who has spent years shepherding gun safety legislation — almost always unsuccessfully — said she introduced the measure on the advice of Senator Chuck Schumer of New York, the

Democratic leader, who reasoned that by offering a narrowly tailored provision, she might get Republican support.

Bump stocks replace a rifle's standard stock, which is the part held against the shoulder, freeing the weapon to slide back and forth rapidly, harnessing the energy from the kickback that shooters feel when the weapon fires. The stock "bumps" back and forth between the shooter's shoulder and trigger finger, causing the rifle to rapidly fire again and again, far faster than an unaided finger can pull a trigger.

In marketing the devices, two Texas companies, Bump Fire Systems and Slide Fire Solutions, were apparently concerned that they would not be legal. But in June 2010, after an inquiry from Slide Fire, the Bureau of Alcohol, Tobacco, Firearms and Explosives, or A.T.F., sent a letter saying that the company's bump stock product "is a firearm part and is not regulated as a firearm under the Gun Control Act or the National Firearms Act."

The Las Vegas gunman fired down on concertgoers from the 32nd floor of a nearby hotel. With his fixed firing positions and distance from his victims, he almost certainly was more lethal because of the conversion kits. But until the shooting, many lawmakers said, they had never heard of bump stocks.

The devices were introduced during the past decade by Bump Fire and Slide Fire, both based in Moran, Tex., near Abilene. Bump Fire's website appeared to be down for much of Wednesday. The company wrote on its Facebook page on Tuesday that its servers had been overwhelmed by "high traffic volume."

Multiple items on Slide Fire's site on Wednesday featured the notice, "Due to extreme high demands, we are currently out of stock."

Bump Fire sells stocks for an AK-47 and an AR-15 for $99.99 each. Slide Fire's stocks are priced between $140 and $300. Neither company responded to a request for comment.

On Gunbroker.com, an auction site for firearms and shooting accessories, at least three dozen listings featuring bump stocks had attracted multiple bids.

Zack Cernok, a Pennsylvania gun owner, was one of those trying to buy a Bump Fire bump stock.

"I don't even have the gun for it, but I want the stock just to have it down the line," he said. "I just like the idea of them and want to see how it feels and if it's worth it — for $100, it's almost not a bad investment to buy it, try it out and sell it if I don't like it."

America Used to Be Good at Gun Control. What Happened?

OPINION | BY ROBERT J. SPITZER | OCT. 3, 2017

IN THE IMMEDIATE AFTERMATH of one of the worst mass shootings in American history, I sought information about what happened by googling "fully automatic weapons" and "Las Vegas." Audio recordings from the scene had picked up the utterly distinctive sound of fully automatic gunfire. (It appears the gun was a modified semi-automatic weapon.) But instead of turning up details of the massacre, the top search results yielded multiple advertisements for sites like "Battlefield Vegas" ("Book Now!") and M.G.V. ("Machine Guns Vegas"), where customers can purchase firing-range time with fully automatic "exclusive Las Vegas gun range packages," according to the second website.

But what happens in Vegas doesn't always stay in Vegas, and sometimes the line between fantasy violence and the real thing disappears.

The horror of the mass shooting in Las Vegas is demarcated by the sheer number of casualties inflicted by a single individual — more than 50 dead and more than 500 injured — made possible by the use of a modified semiautomatic weapon or weapons, meaning those that fire a continuous stream of bullets by depressing the trigger. Semiautomatic weapons fire one bullet with each pull of the trigger.

The Vegas shooting stands out because, for all of the gun crimes committed annually in America, fully automatic or modified semiautomatic weapons virtually never play a role, thanks to America's first significant national gun law. America's close-up experience with automatic weapons nearly a century ago culminated in the adoption of the National Firearms Act of 1934.

Prohibition and later the Great Depression fueled the rise of gangsterism that spread unregulated but powerful weapons developed for warfare, including the Tommy gun ("the gun that made the twenties roar") and the Browning automatic rifle. By the start of the 1930s, more than half of the states had sharply regulated or barred such fully automatic weapons. In the summer of 1934, President Franklin D. Roosevelt signed into law a measure to bring these and other gangster weapons and equipment, like sawed-off shotguns and silencers, under federal control. The new law required an extensive and intensive background check, fingerprinting, registration with a national database and payment of a $200 fee.

The effectiveness of this measure, amended slightly in 1968 and 1986 to ban possession of full automatic weapons, or machine guns, manufactured after that year, put a lid on the spread of these weapons. According to government records, today only about a half-million such guns are in civilian hands. (To comply with the 1986 law expanding the 1934 Firearms Act, citizens are barred from purchasing any fully automatic weapon made after 1986. That includes weapons manufactured to fire in full auto mode and those altered to fire in full auto.) Of guns used in crimes subject to law enforcement tracing, only three of every 1,000 were machine guns.

This success story notwithstanding, mass shootings are on the rise, facilitated by weapons that can still deliver plenty of destructive power. In a study of mass shootings over a 30-year period, more than a third were committed with semiautomatic assault weapons (there are perhaps five million such weapons legally owned as of 2016).

Yet even as mass shootings rise, most of the nation has gone in the opposite direction, following the contrary notion that somehow we would be better off with fewer gun laws and more guns. For example, at the start of the 1980s, 19 states banned concealed gun carrying by civilians entirely, and 29 states had great discretion over whether to grant carry permits. Only one state, Vermont, imposed no permitting restrictions. As of this year, only nine states retain discretion over whether to grant permits (New York is one).

In 29 states, permits must be issued to applicants unless they are felons or mentally incompetent, and 12 states have abolished permitting entirely. In 24 states, no gun training is required to carry a gun. Congress is now considering a bill, called concealed carry reciprocity, to require that every state's concealed-carry standard be accepted by every other state. This would have the effect of undercutting states with stricter laws since it would impose a national lowest-common-denominator standard.

A different effort to thwart a successful gun law is afoot in Congress: The House of Representatives was poised to pass a bill to remove the 1934 N.F.A. background check, registration and fee requirements one must satisfy to own a gun silencer (also called "suppressors"). Because of the Las Vegas shooting, that bill is now shelved, but when things die down, expect its progress to resume.

The reason for the change? Advocates argue that silencers are almost never used in crimes, and that silencers help protect the gun users' hearing. Yet the very reason silencers were originally subject to registration regulations was because they were used in crimes, and because their chief utility was to conceal gun crimes and illegal hunting with guns. And while the modern idea of protecting the shooter's hearing is laudable, the more effective method for doing so would be to subsidize gun owners' ownership of proper hearing-protection devices, precisely so that innocent bystanders can tell where hostile fire is coming from — whether in the woods during hunting season or in the killing grounds of downtown Las Vegas.

The gun issue is virtually the only one where the default response is increasingly to shrug and say that laws don't matter, since bad people do bad things, so why bother with new ones? That facile and false logic jumps over an obvious question: Shouldn't the government do more to keep highly destructive weapons from the wrong hands? Sure, it's a politically fraught question, but it's no less important.

Admittedly, mass shooters tend to be individuals with little or no serious criminal past, making them hard to identify before they commit these acts. Recent research has suggested a high correlation with their abuse of intimate partners or family members, but a vast majority of abusers will never pick up a gun and shoot a bunch of people.

Still, many mass shooters do give indications of impending violence to those around them, and only a few states have any measures in place to pick up on that. New York, as it happens, is one, with its extensive character background investigation for pistol permit applicants (a process I underwent). Other states would do well to follow its lead.

If we can't settle on sensible gun regulations in the wake of Sandy Hook or San Bernardino or Orlando or now Las Vegas (or Aurora or Columbine or Virginia Tech before them), when will we? Maybe the answer will emerge when the nation's cumulative gun violence toxicity level reaches a critical tipping point. Are we there yet?

ROBERT SPITZER is a political scientist at SUNY Cortland and the author of five books on gun policy, including "Guns Across America" and "The Politics of Gun Control."

Trump Says Issue Is Mental Health, Not Gun Control

BY PETER BAKER | NOV. 6, 2017

WASHINGTON — As Americans struggled Monday to make sense once again of the mass shootings plaguing the United States, President Trump sought to steer the national conversation to questions about the mental capacity of those pulling the triggers, not the weapons themselves.

Mr. Trump, who has presented himself since his presidential campaign as a strong supporter of the Second Amendment's right to bear arms, weighed in from Asia hours after a man clad in black, wearing a ballistic vest and armed with a military-style rifle, mowed down parishioners in a small-town church in Texas, killing 26 and injuring many more.

"I think that mental health is your problem here," Mr. Trump told reporters at a news conference in Japan, the first stop on his 12-day overseas trip. Based on preliminary reports, the gunman in Sutherland Springs, Tex., was a "very deranged individual," he said. "We have a lot of mental health problems in our country, as do other countries."

"But this isn't a guns situation," Mr. Trump added. "I mean, we could go into it, but it's a little bit soon to go into it. But fortunately, somebody else had a gun that was shooting in the opposite direction, otherwise it would have been — as bad it was — it would have been much worse. But this is a mental health problem at the highest level. It's a very, very sad event."

Mr. Trump's answer to the fifth-deadliest mass shooting in modern American history was much the same as his answer to the deadliest mass shooting in modern American history barely a month ago in Las Vegas. For gun-rights supporters, the focus on mental health has become the standard response to shooting massacres, just as more gun control has been the standard response from the other side of the ideological divide.

As more information became available on Monday, it turned out that the gunman in Texas, identified as Devin P. Kelley, 26, should have already been barred from purchasing firearms because of a domestic violence conviction. While serving in the Air Force, he was convicted of two charges in 2012 by a court-martial after assaulting his wife and breaking his infant stepson's skull. But the Air Force never entered his name in the National Instant Criminal Background Check System.

The current law also bans gun sales to anyone "adjudicated mental defective or involuntarily committed to a mental institution or incompetent to handle own affairs." But the database relies on states to transmit such information to the federal government, and compliance is patchy depending on the state.

Mr. Trump made no suggestion on Monday that he would follow up his assessment of the Texas shooting with any concrete policy proposals. After the Las Vegas massacre, he indicated that he would consider new restrictions on so-called bump stock firearm accessories that can convert a semiautomatic rifle into an automatic weapon, but so far he has not followed up.

Shortly after becoming president, Mr. Trump signed legislation repealing a regulation enacted by President Barack Obama intended to add the names of mentally ill Americans registered with the Social Security Administration to the database for gun purchase background checks. The regulation, a response by Mr. Obama in part to the 2012 school shooting in Newtown, Conn., would have affected those unable to work because of severe mental impairment and unable to manage their own Social Security financial benefits.

In February, both houses of Congress passed a resolution revoking the resolution. Mr. Trump's aides said at the time that he signed it because he did not want to deprive law-abiding citizens of their constitutional rights.

Critics said Mr. Trump's action in February belied his words on Monday.

On Monday in Tokyo, President Trump addressed the Sunday shooting at a Texas church, steering the national conversation to questions about the mental capacity of those pulling the triggers.

"If this is a mental health problem, it begs the question of why we let people with mental health problems have access to firearms," said Cecilia Muñoz, who was Mr. Obama's domestic policy adviser.

She acknowledged that it was tricky determining who had a mental illness serious enough to make them a risk and therefore worthy of inclusion in the background check database. "It is controversial," she said. "It's not easy to figure out where you draw the line. But it is important to draw a line."

Others argued that targeting mentally ill people in a broad way would be unfair to millions of Americans who posed no threat to anyone and would not solve the problem.

Jeffrey Swanson, a psychiatry and behavioral sciences professor at Duke University, said a study of 82,000 people given a diagnosis of serious mental illnesses in Florida between 2002 and 2011 found that they were no more likely to use a gun to harm others than the rest of the population — about 213 crimes annually per 100,000 people compared with 217.

"There's this horrible mass shooting, and it's so disturbing and so frightening and so irrational and people want an explanation for it," he said. "Someone who's capable of going out and massacring so many strangers, they can't be like you and me, they must be mentally ill. And then that gets overgeneralized."

Mr. Swanson said Mr. Trump's reference to mental health was "a huge dodge" to avoid a gun control debate. But Mr. Swanson said that rather than focusing on mental health generally, policymakers should focus on violent history as a better predictor of gun violence. "We don't have to tolerate this," he said. "We can live in a less violent society."

When a Gun Maker
Proposed Gun Control

BY DANNY HAKIM | FEB. 9, 2018

WHEN DEVIN PATRICK KELLEY took a Ruger AR-556 semiautomatic assault rifle to the First Baptist Church in Sutherland Springs, Tex., last November, he brought 15 high-capacity magazines that each contained 30 bullets.

How many did he empty?

"All of them," a Texas law enforcement official said at a news conference in the days after the massacre.

If William B. Ruger Sr., the co-founder of the gun maker Sturm, Ruger & Company, had had his way, Mr. Kelley's firepower might have been much diminished. In 1989, Mr. Ruger proposed a ban on high-capacity magazines, which led a smaller rival to call Sturm, Ruger "the Benedict Arnold of the gun industry."

Mr. Ruger once said that he was open even to waiting periods for

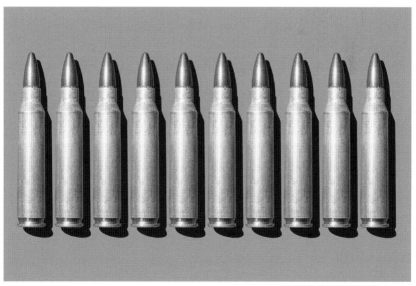

JENS MORTENSEN FOR THE NEW YORK TIMES

handgun purchases. "If the truth be known, I see no real harm in the concept," he said, but cautioned, "the trouble is, where does it end?"

Mr. Ruger was certainly not a cheerleader for gun control. But considering the tide of mass shootings and gridlock on the issue of guns, his willingness to compromise is worth revisiting.

Mr. Ruger, a Brooklyn-born gun designer, took an inventor's interest in guns after his father gave him a rifle at age 12. A 1981 profile in The New York Times reported that he read everything he could about guns at the New York Public Library and "studied gun metallurgy, gun mechanisms, gun designs" and "came to regard the gun as a uniquely engineered tool."

He also liked to recount how he once revealed to guests at a Manhattan cocktail party what he did for a living.

"When you mention you're in the gun business, people look shocked," he said. "They infer that you have an utter disregard for human life, which is preposterous."

He said at the time, "There's so much hostility, so many people stimulated to violence. But to be talking about gun legislation as a cure for this is ridiculous."

His position appeared to evolve. A series of mass shootings captured headlines in the following years. Among them, an unemployed security guard named James Oliver Huberty used an Uzi semiautomatic rifle, a 12-gauge shotgun and a 9-millimeter semiautomatic pistol during a 1984 rampage at a McDonald's in California that left 21 dead and 19 wounded. In 1991, an unemployment merchant seaman, George J. Hennard, shot 22 people dead at a cafeteria in Killeen, Tex., and injured another 20.

With momentum building for gun control, Mr. Ruger's move was partly tactical. He and his allies wanted "to take a responsible position to head off any further restrictions that might even have banned all semiautomatic firearms," Robert L. Wilson wrote in the book "Ruger and His Guns."

From the gun industry's point of view, Mr. Ruger's stance is a cautionary tale. If he aimed to forestall a ban on assault weapons, in the end, both assault weapons and high-capacity magazines were banned through a 1994 measure signed by President Bill Clinton. The ban expired in 2004.

"You give people who are truly anti-gun an inch, and they'll take a mile," Stephen L. Sanetti, a former Ruger executive, told The Hartford Courant in 2013. Mr. Sanetti, who now runs the National Shooting Sports Foundation, a lobby group, declined to comment through a spokesman.

In an email, Kevin B. Reid Sr., the vice president and general counsel of Sturm, Ruger, said, "As I am sure you can appreciate, Mr. Ruger died many years ago and folks who were around and worked with him directly are long gone."

"Indeed, none of the Ruger family has been involved in the day-to-day operation of the business for more than a decade," he added. (In 2006, the family made a large sale of its holdings back to the company.) "As such, there really isn't anyone who can speak to his comments or views."

Gunmakers are not proposing gun control anymore. After the 2012 Sandy Hook massacre led to the deaths of 20 first graders and six adults, Senator Pat Toomey, a Pennsylvania Republican, was a co-sponsor of legislation that would have required universal background checks.

"I'm a big believer in the Second Amendment, I'm a gun owner and take my son shooting," he said in an interview. But at the same time, he said, "I think it's completely reasonable to make it more difficult for those who do not have a legitimate right to a firearm to obtain them."

The legislation, which was also sponsored by Senator Joe Manchin, a West Virginia Democrat, failed.

"You know, the N.R.A. used to be very big supporters of mine, institutionally; they are not so much anymore," Mr. Toomey said. "I will say honestly, a vast majority of Pennsylvanians agree with my approach on background checks, so on balance, I don't think it hurt me politically."

The N.R.A., which did not return calls for comment, has lately been pushing to compel states that do not allow concealed carry permits to honor permits issued by other states. It is also trying to deregulate silencers.

John Feinblatt, president of Everytown for Gun Safety, a gun control group backed by Michael R. Bloomberg, said his group spent more money lobbying states than the federal government. Restrictions on bump stocks, the device that makes semiautomatic weapons more like machine guns, faltered in Washington after they were used in the Las Vegas massacre. But bans have been enacted in Massachusetts and New Jersey.

"The way to move Congress is to show where the people stand on this issue, and you do that most effectively through state ballots and state legislation," Mr. Feinblatt said, likening the approach to the way gay rights advocates methodically advanced marriage rights through state legislatures.

Many other western democracies have far tighter gun control laws. The rate of homicides with guns in the United States is 16 times higher than it is in Germany, 6.6 times higher than it is in Canada and more than 30 times higher than in Australia or Britain, according to data collected by the United Nations Office on Drugs and Crime.

Twenty-six people died in the Sutherland Springs shooting, including the pastor's 14-year-old daughter and a pregnant woman, while another 20 were injured by a gun bearing the Ruger name. If he were alive today, America's most outspoken gun maker would likely have had something to say.

Right and Left React to the Deepening Divide Over Gun Control

BY ANNA DUBENKO | FEB. 22, 2018

The political news cycle is fast, and keeping up can be overwhelming. Trying to find differing perspectives worth your time is even harder. That's why we have scoured the internet for political writing from the right and left that you might not have seen.

FROM THE RIGHT

David French in National Review:

> *"When facing the big questions about guns — such as whether America should 'ban' an entire category of weapons (such as 'assault weapons') — it's better, I think, to go back to the first principles embodied in the Second Amendment."*

If you're looking for an argument that explains why keeping assault weapons legal is so important to some supporters of the Second Amendment, look no further than Mr. French's column. Rooting his reasoning in Justice Antonin Scalia's writing on the subject, Mr. French explains how any gun-control efforts must be evaluated based on these "twin purposes" of that amendment: "the amendment protects a person's individual inherent right of self-defense and empowers the collective obligation to defend liberty against state tyranny."

A. Barton Hinkle in Reason:

> *"Collective punishment should offend not just gun owners, but any American who believes in individual responsibility and due process."*

Mr. Hinkle proposes a gun control solution that protects gun rights: the "gun violence restraining order." Such an order, he writes, would allow friends and family who suspect that someone may pose a danger to himself or others a way to alert law enforcement and prevent that person from acquiring a gun. The idea is particularly appealing to Mr. Hinkle because it avoids punishing the majority of law-abiding gun owners by tightening gun laws across the board.

FROM THE LEFT
Rebecca Klein in HuffPost:

> *"There's an abundance of evidence suggesting that more school security means more vulnerable students getting funneled at an early age into the criminal justice system."*

A possible consequence to the proposal to make schools safer by adding more police officers is a potential negative effect on minority students. As Ms. Klein points out, black children are already more likely to be arrested on school grounds for relatively minor infractions like vandalism. When you add more police officers at schools, she writes, the "school-to-prison pipeline" only grows.

Osita Nwanevu in Slate:

> *"That ultimately may be what galls conservatives about Stoneman Douglas' teens most of all: They suggest the notions underpinning our status quo gun policy are infantile, beneath even them despite their youth."*

Mr. Nwanevu addresses those conservative commentators who have criticized the Florida teenagers who are speaking out on gun control. If any gun control measures result from this tragedy, he writes, "we'll have the kids, and only the kids, to thank." Moreover, referring to the conservative columnist Ben Shapiro, he points out that "young, supposedly precocious voices like his have proved deeply important to the modern conservative movement since at least 1960."

FINALLY, FROM THE CENTER

Lili Loofbourow in The Week:

> *"Uncomfortable confrontations like these, in which there is no conversion or resolution or repentance on either side, are real and instructive. We need to see many more of them."*

Sometimes the best debate is the one that has no clear "winner," Ms. Loofbourow writes. She compares the difficult, and at times contentious town hall-style meeting held by CNN with the listening session held by President Trump and Secretary of Education Betsy DeVos. The CNN gathering she argues, "gave grieving students, parents, and teachers in Florida a forum to confront lawmakers and corporate interests as equals." She also points out that it is jarring to see "citizens treat their public servants as public servants," a structure that perhaps allowed the politicians to speak to one another in ways we are unused to.

The editorial board of Bloomberg View:

> *"Binary choices in public debates are rarely helpful. But too many Americans have allowed bad faith and fanaticism to hold this field for far too long."*

The editorial board of Bloomberg View is heartened by the message of the Florida students demanding change on gun laws: "You are responsible." They write that adults should take a cue from these young people and enact "sensible gun regulation" including universal background checks.

Gun Smoke and Mirrors

OPINION | BY ANDREW ROSENTHAL | FEB. 27, 2018

AS I WATCHED President Trump blathering to a group of governors on Monday about throwing people who have not committed a crime into mental hospitals to prevent mass shootings at schools, I recalled a country where I once lived in which the government had that power — the Soviet Union.

From the mid-1960s until the fall of Soviet Communism, the Kremlin employed the notion of "sluggish schizophrenia" — dreamed up by the Mengele-like psychiatrist Andrei Snezhnevsky — to imprison people on the ground that they were on their way to becoming insane.

Rejected by most civilized nations as a transparent fraud, sluggish schizophrenia was used against dissidents and other citizens who simply dared to seek exit visas. When I worked in Moscow as a reporter in the mid-1980s, I knew an Estonian man who was committed twice for refusing to enter the Red Army during the war in Afghanistan, an act of sanity. It was a literal Catch-22.

Now comes Trump, urging the nation's governors to return to a time when he said the states could "nab" people and throw them in a padded room because "something was off."

In fact, the law has required court-ratified findings of actual mental illness for involuntary commitment since around 1881, said Dr. Paul Appelbaum, a professor at Columbia University's medical school. "It was never the case that people could be involuntary committed for being a little odd, or even for that matter thought to be dangerous to other people unless they had evidence of mental illness," he said.

I'm not bringing this up to suggest that Trump is a disciple of Snezhnevsky, despite his bizarre affinity for Kremlin autocracy, or merely to point out that the president was once again making things up. Rather, it is an example of the incoherent, insincere and inadequate ways in which the president and others on the right are suddenly claiming to be dedicated to addressing the nation's epidemic of gun violence.

They are playing a cynical game of misdirection.

It is tragic that in recent decades, states have closed mental hospitals and thrown people into prisons when they should be receiving psychiatric care. But that has little to do with gun violence — in or out of schools, on a small or mass scale.

The gun-control group Everytown for Gun Safety studied 133 acts of mass murder committed between January 2009 and July 2015 and found that only one of the murderers had been "prohibited by federal law from possessing guns due to severe mental illness." In only 11 percent of the cases did the group find "evidence that concerns about the mental health of the shooter had been brought to the attention of a medical practitioner, school official or legal authority."

Similarly, the president's newfound support for banning bump stocks, which allow semiautomatic weapons to be fired nearly as

ZACK WITTMAN FOR THE NEW YORK TIMES

A semiautomatic rifle for sale at the Florida Gun Show in Tampa on Sunday.

rapidly as automatic ones, is fine, on the surface. But bump stocks could have been banned at any time before or since a killer used them to murder 58 people in Las Vegas last fall, and Trump has done nothing to make it happen.

Some politicians — so far not including Trump or the Republican leadership in Congress — are calling for raising the age to buy a semiautomatic weapon to 21 from 18. (The person charged with the murders in Parkland, Fla., this month was 19.)

There should be such a law, on a national basis and not state by state, but Everytown found that only 5 percent of the mass shooters it studied were under 20. And of course, mass shooting victims account for a tiny percentage of the Americans gunned down every year. A majority of children killed by guns are killed by accident, or by their own hand, or by adults, with weapons legally obtained by adults.

Trump also chimed in on calls from the right to arm more teachers and train them to shoot would-be killers. It's an absurd and dangerous idea. Highly trained police officers frequently miss their targets, even at close range, in the heat of the moment. Having armed civilians at a shooting scene would just make their jobs harder.

The real problem with gun violence is not about mental hospitals, armed teachers, bump stocks or age requirements. The real problem is that there are far too many firearms in America — more than 300 million, according to Congress. They are too easy to obtain and they are becoming ever more lethal.

But the gun lobby, led by the National Rifle Association, has stopped every effort to reduce the number and lethality of firearms, a crusade that seems as much or more about expanding the markets for firearms makers than about constitutional principles.

Banning the possession of semiautomatic weapons by civilians would be a better approach. So would repealing lax concealed-carry laws, stand-your-ground laws and other rules that are proliferating around America to make it easier to shoot someone and get away with it.

The risk is that the passage of a few partial measures will take our eyes off the bigger picture and drain the energy out of the demands for change led by young people after the Parkland slaughter. That is what the gun lobby is counting on.

Republican and Democratic Lawmakers Get Facts Wrong on Gun Policy

BY LINDA QIU | MARCH 1, 2018

PRESIDENT TRUMP discussed potential solutions to curb gun violence on Wednesday during a televised meeting with a bipartisan group of lawmakers.

The president strayed from the facts during his remarks, as The New York Times reported previously. Here is a look at the claims made during the session by other lawmakers — Republicans and Democrats — that may have strayed from the facts or otherwise require some additional context.

"This is when the 10-year assault weapon ban was in — how incidents and deaths dropped. When it ended, you see it going up." — Senator Dianne Feinstein

This needs context.

In the past, Ms. Feinstein has referenced an analysis by Louis Klarevas, a lecturer at the University of Massachusetts Boston, that found the assault weapons ban drastically reduced gun massacres.

But it's difficult to directly link declines in crime or gun violence to any specific law, given the limited scope and loopholes in each one, according to most experts and research.

As The Times has previously reported:

> The 1994 ban on assault weapons has become a particular and recent subject of intense debate. The N.R.A. has cited a 2004 analysis funded by the Justice Department to argue that the "ban could not be credited with any reduction in crime."

On the other hand, Senator Dianne Feinstein, Democrat of California, has claimed in a Twitter post that "the number of gun massacres fell by 37%" while the ban was in place.

Christopher Koper, a professor at George Mason University in Fairfax, Va., and the lead author of the study that is cited by the N.R.A., has repeatedly said that the ban had mixed effects and final results would not be immediately evident.

"My work is often cited in misleading ways that don't give the full picture," Mr. Koper said Thursday in an email. "These laws can modestly reduce shootings overall" and reduce the number and severity of mass shootings.

"These shooters typically are males. They're white and they're suicidal." — Senator Steve Daines, Republican of Montana

True.

A database maintained by Mother Jones, a progressive magazine, shows that 95 out of 97 mass shootings from 1982 to 2018 involved male gunmen. Fifty-five were committed by white men.

"The states that have these background checks, they have a 38 percent lower domestic homicide rate — this is domestic violence." — Senator Amy Klobuchar, Democrat of Minnesota

Causation is not clear.

Ms. Klobuchar is probably referring to a report from Everytown for Gun Safety, a gun control advocacy group, that claims "38 percent fewer women" are "shot to death by intimate partners" in states that require background checks for all handgun sales.

This analysis, however, does not account for other factors that contribute to domestic violence, leading other researchers to question the sweeping conclusion about background checks.

April Zeoli, a professor at Michigan State University who studies intimate partner violence, called the Everytown estimate a "back of the napkin" calculation.

Ms. Zeoli's research has found that state laws restricting access to firearms for people who have been convicted of domestic violence result in declines in intimate partner homicides; specifically, 11 percent from laws that mandate buyers to get a permit whether they're purchasing from licensed or private dealers, she said. (Other research also shows this.)

Unlike Everytown, Ms. Zeoli also looked at state domestic violence laws, poverty and divorce rates, average amounts of public assistance, educational attainment gaps between men and women, homicides not related to domestic violence, percentage of suicides by firearms as a proxy for gun ownership rates and law enforcement availability.

"Those are areas where there are no guns. The reason I carry a concealed firearm everywhere I go is because I don't know where those gun-free zones are, that I may walking through at the mall, or at the doughnut shop, or wherever I might be." — Representative John Rutherford, Republican of Florida

This needs context.

As Mr. Rutherford and Mr. Trump discussed concealed-carry laws, Mr. Trump said, "You're not allowed concealed in a gun-free zone." The exchange highlights how amorphous the term "gun-free zone" has become.

Federal law prohibits firearms in grade schools, but makes explicit exceptions for security personnel and instructional purposes (hunting classes, for example). So, Mr. Rutherford is wrong to state that there are never guns in "gun-free zones."

Furthermore, at least eight states allow concealed carry for teachers at grade schools, and two others have eased restrictions, according to the Giffords Law Center, a gun control advocacy group.

Private businesses may also ban civilian use of firearms on their premises, but state laws vary on how and on the extent to which a business can opt out.

Texas has very specific requirements for the signs businesses put up to indicate that they do not allow firearms on their properties. (For example, they must be in both English and Spanish.) North Carolina requires signs to be "conspicuous," while Florida has no explicit rules. Florida is one of 23 states that require business owners to allow guns in cars parked on company property.

"People just want to dismiss concealed-carry permits. They do actually increase safety." — Representative Steve Scalise, Republican of Louisiana

This is disputed.

When asked what data Mr. Scalise was referring to, a spokesman told The Times, "Since the early '90s, the significant increase in the issuance of concealed-carry permits by states has been accompanied by a significant drop in violent crime rates — and that includes millions of new permits being issued in the last decade or so."

The spokesman cited the work of John R. Lott Jr., an economist and gun rights advocate whose book "More Guns, Less Crime" makes the case that "passing concealed-handgun laws deters violent crime." But Mr. Lott's findings have been questioned by other academics.

In 2005, a panel at the National Academies of Sciences, Engineering and Medicine concluded that "no link between right-to-carry laws and changes in crime is apparent in the raw data, even in the initial sample."

Other researchers have reached an opposite conclusion. In a 2017 study, John Donohue, a professor at Stanford Law School, found that states that adopted right-to-carry laws saw an increase in violent crime.

Once Again, Push for Gun Control Collides With Political Reality

BY CARL HULSE | FEB. 28, 2018

WASHINGTON — Here's how significant things don't get done in Washington even in a moment of crisis and opportunity.

The president throws out a hodgepodge of ideas, thoroughly confusing both sides about what he really supports. Senate Republicans, grappling for an answer that responds to public clamor but doesn't alienate their conservative base, would prefer instead to focus on a small fix unlikely to satisfy many people even if it could overcome internal divisions. House Republicans say they will wait to see what the Senate does — though history has shown that can be a very long wait. Democrats push for a broad debate that Republicans want nothing to do with.

That's where Washington stands now on the subject of new gun legislation after the school shooting in Parkland, Fla. Despite immense public pressure in part from students who escaped the attack, the outlook for any consequential action remains dim as the president and lawmakers diverge on how best to respond.

President Trump upended the discussion on Wednesday during a bipartisan White House meeting with lawmakers. He seemed to side more with Democrats than Republicans on gun rights, chided fellow Republicans for fearing the National Rifle Association and even suggested that guns should be summarily confiscated from suspects who raise red flags, forcing them to go to court to regain them. Such an approach toward gun rights runs counter to Republican dogma, as did other suggestions that the president made.

But the meeting was very similar to an earlier White House session in which the president seemed to join with Democrats on divisive immigration policy only to later reverse course, leaving the parties at an impasse. Members of both parties expressed skepticism on

Wednesday that the White House meeting would lead to a break-through. They even suggested that it could prove counterproductive by forcing the gun lobby to dig in its heels and by making Republican leaders unwilling to push ahead given the possibility of glaring divisions with Mr. Trump. Officials said the next issue on the Senate agenda was likely to be a rollback of banking regulations, not increased gun control.

Mr. Trump's stream-of-consciousness display was just the latest wrinkle in the contentious struggle over gun safety. The most widely backed response to the Parkland shooting would provide new incentives for public agencies to submit information that could disqualify prospective gun buyers to the National Instant Criminal Background Check System, an action most agree is modest at best.

Even though they support it themselves, leading Democrats consider that proposal, sponsored by Senator John Cornyn of Texas, the No. 2 Republican, to be woefully insufficient given the scope of the mass shootings.

"The Cornyn bill is kind of a fig leaf," said Senator Claire McCaskill of Missouri, one of the Democrats up for re-election in a state that President Trump carried in 2016.

To Democrats, the fact that the N.R.A. is not opposed to the proposal is prima facie evidence that it falls short. They are demanding a more robust debate over a series of gun initiatives, notably what they call a "universal" background check system that would cover all gun transactions in the country. That plan is opposed by the gun lobby but was seemingly endorsed by Mr. Trump, putting him at odds not only with the gun advocacy group that strongly backed him, but with many congressional Republicans, as well.

Senator Christopher S. Murphy, Democrat of Connecticut and an author, with Mr. Cornyn, of the more limited background check bill, equated taking up his own legislation without allowing consideration of alternatives to "slamming the door in the face of all these kids who are demanding change."

"I think it is imperative that we rise to the moment," Mr. Murphy said.

Mr. Trump told lawmakers they should use a broader bipartisan background check measure that failed in 2013 after the school shooting in Newtown, Conn., as the basis for a comprehensive measure that could take in many proposals, including the Cornyn plan, new mental health provisions and added security for schools. He urged backers of a renewed ban on assault weapons to make their case to the authors of the legislation and said he would welcome the opportunity to enact one sweeping bill to combat mass shootings. But Congress has for years been unable to make even incremental headway on new gun buying limits, let alone the type of multifaceted plan called for by the president.

Democrats would like to persuade Senator Mitch McConnell, Republican of Kentucky and the majority leader, to allow votes on major gun control proposals, a plan that could throw the Senate into a full-blown showdown over competing initiatives. But Mr. McConnell is never one to rush into a fight that divides his own party if he can help it. While Mr. McConnell has been quiet about his intentions, Mr. Cornyn opened the door to that possibility of a wider debate provided it could get to passage of his bill at a minimum.

"We can set up a situation where they can vote on those amendments," he said. "What I don't want to do is leave here this week and go back home to Texas and say we failed to do anything to try to address these tragedies."

As lawmakers quibbled about how to proceed, some of the multiple proposals promoted by Mr. Trump were falling by the wayside.

Republican lawmakers seem uninterested in plans to raise the age to buy all guns to 21. The idea of arming teachers was also getting a cold reception. Among plans circulating that could draw bipartisan support was a measure that would prevent those on federal no-fly lists from buying guns, though that approach has met Republican resistance in the past.

Hoping to skirt a divisive debate, Republicans preferred to focus on other remedies, like improving general school safety, while pointing to law enforcement failures surrounding the Parkland shooting.

Democrats remained doubtful that Republicans would be willing to buck the N.R.A., particularly in an election year, but said it would be an imperative for legislative success.

"You can't solve this problem and please the N.R.A.," said Senator Chuck Schumer of New York, the Democratic leader. "Our Republican colleagues need to learn that."

Given longstanding political conflict over the issue, many lawmakers in both parties anticipate the push for new laws will likely fall apart as so many others have in the aftermath of mass shootings.

If that is the outcome, the determined high school students and their allies who have helped drive the debate to this point seem unlikely to let the issue go. Maybe the difference this time isn't that Congress will act, but it is that those pushing Congress will not allow lawmakers to so quickly move on after they don't.

Support for Gun Control Seems Strong. But It May Be Softer Than It Looks.

BY MARGOT SANGER-KATZ | MARCH 24, 2018

WHEN YOU ASK Americans in a poll whether they support universal background checks for gun purchases, huge majorities say yes.

Ask them for a specific vote for such a legal change, and that support drops off.

In recent years, there have been three true tests of this question. In Washington State and Nevada, voters said yes. In Maine, they said no. Ballot measures in all three earned a much smaller vote share than the initial polling suggested.

The results illustrate the political challenges facing the student-led activists who are marching in Washington and other cities this weekend to push for stronger gun laws.

While a wide range of gun control laws appear popular in polls, support may soften once details emerge and they're subjected to a robust political debate. In survey after survey, background checks are the most popular gun control measure, with support frequently over 80 percent. A recent Quinnipiac poll, taken after the deadly shootings last month at Marjory Stoneman Douglas High in Parkland, Fla., had support at 97 percent. Background checks are popular among Democrats and Republicans, gun owners and those without guns.

Many gun measures get high marks in polls. In 2016, The New York Times asked Morning Consult to survey voters about 29 possible gun laws. Only one, which would have required gun owners to demonstrate a "genuine need" before being allowed to have a weapon, garnered less than majority endorsement. Our results are roughly consistent with a range of polls from a number of outlets, which show that many gun control ideas are popular in surveys.

But political consultants who have worked on ballot measures say that it can often be easy for opponents of gun laws to chip away at very strong initial public support for a given policy. That's a dynamic that is true of all ballot measures, where voters must be persuaded to overcome a normal bias in favor of the status quo.

"You're not asking people what is your sentiment," said Zach Silk, the president of the public policy firm Civic Ventures, who led the 2014 background check effort in Washington and was a consultant for Nevada's initiative in 2016. "It's getting them to think about what system they want."

More broadly worded polling questions, such as those that ask people if they value controls on gun ownership or protection of gun rights, show a public that is much more closely divided. Americans remain split in their views of the National Rifle Association, the country's most prominent gun rights group. Mr. Silk said he likes to look at those responses, and support for an assault weapons ban, as good approximations of overall public support for gun restrictions, because all three questions force people to contend with the inherent trade-offs between enhanced safety and restrictions in rights.

He said recent surveys, which show growing support for more restrictive laws on guns and assault weapons and declining support for the N.R.A., feed his optimism that the country may be experiencing a "phase shift" on guns.

But David Farmer, who led the Maine effort for universal background checks in 2016, said that supporters of gun rights can be particularly persuasive once a concrete proposal is unveiled. In Maine, polling support for the measure declined between introduction and the final vote, before failing, 52-48.

"We know for a fact we lost the argument at the kitchen table and the bar and the bowling alley," he said. "The gun enthusiasts were talking to their friends and relatives and neighbors. They felt about it in a way that was so passionate that they won those one-on-one encounters, and they were very successful in bringing in people to their side."

The enthusiasm of gun rights activists doesn't show up just in personal conversations. Over the last few decades, they have been more likely to speak to their legislators or give money to gun-related political groups, according to research from the Pew Research Center. Those actions have sent a signal to legislators that there is robust opposition even to laws that show strong public support in polls.

John Feinblatt, the president of Everytown for Gun Safety, a group that favors stricter gun laws, thinks the energy imbalance is shifting. He said the group's donations, membership and Instagram follows have all risen since the Parkland shootings, a suggestion, he said, that members of the public who back Everytown's agenda are increasing the intensity of their support.

He also noted a string of recent state legislative successes on gun restrictions for domestic abusers, including some in Republican-led states, and the recent passage of a law in Florida that allows judges to temporarily confiscate guns from people who are judged a threat. (On Friday, an N.R.A. spokesman declined to offer the organization's views of public opinion on gun measures.)

Mr. Farmer said he is also optimistic that his side can do a better job of persuading voters in the future. He said he's particularly heartened by the recent groundswell of activism by young Americans. He said he sees parallels between their energy and that of the opposition.

Several polls since the Parkland shootings show a rise in support for gun restrictions, including some that go beyond universal background checks. President Trump's proposal to arm schoolteachers has received more lukewarm support — with fewer than 45 percent of the public supporting it in two recent surveys. It will take some time to see whether the trends hold.

America Passed Gun Control in 1968. Can It Happen Again?

OPINION | BY JASON SOKOL | MARCH 22, 2018

DAYS AFTER A horrifying act of violence, a Democrat from Connecticut stood on the Senate floor and declared, "I hope that this brutal, senseless killing will shock the Congress into backing me in this fight to take the guns from the hands of assassins and murderers." The senator was not Chris Murphy of Connecticut, who has become Capitol Hill's leading voice for gun safety legislation. And the act of violence was not the kind of mass shooting that haunts our nation in the 21st century. It was 50 years ago, after the assassination of the Rev. Dr. Martin Luther King Jr., that one of Senator Murphy's predecessors, Thomas Dodd, issued this stirring plea.

King was murdered in Memphis on April 4, 1968. That killing, together with the assassination of Robert F. Kennedy two months later, spurred the passage of the Gun Control Act that year. It was the first time since the 1930s that the federal government had passed a major gun control bill.

We are now witnessing the emergence of the most passionate movement for gun control since 1968. The country's ordeal half a century ago illustrates that horrific episodes of gun violence do not themselves prompt legislative action; only the sustained pressure of an energized populace can do that. The students of Marjory Stoneman Douglas High School in Parkland, Fla., surely grasp this truth.

Those who organized for gun control in 1968 ultimately obtained a piece of legislation that President Lyndon Johnson admitted was "not nearly enough." The question remains whether the eloquent and indefatigable Stoneman Douglas students, and their millions of allies across the country who will take to the streets in protest this weekend, can push legislators further.

After the assassination of President John F. Kennedy in 1963, advocates of gun control tried to bring legislation to the Senate floor. Dodd often led the charge. At first, he worked with the arms manufacturers in Connecticut and the National Rifle Association. But the N.R.A. grew more extreme over the course of the decade and began to oppose almost all regulatory legislation. Dodd's bills never made it out of Senate committees.

By 1967, opinion polls found widespread support for gun control, even among gun owners. One of the prime reasons was racism: Whites feared black people with guns, whether they were Black Panthers or urban rioters. In the spring of 1967, the California Legislature passed the Mulford Act, which outlawed the open display of guns and was aimed at restraining the Black Panther Party.

But such legislative action had become increasingly rare. On April 4, 1968, one hour before James Earl Ray aimed his rifle at the balcony of the Lorraine Motel in Memphis, the Senate Judiciary Committee deadlocked on a proposal to regulate gun sales (it banned mail-order and interstate gun sales, though it exempted rifles and shotguns). Four senators had been absent from the meeting. At another meeting of the committee two days later, they tipped the balance in favor of this amendment, which had been offered by Dodd. The measure was added to the Safe Streets Act, which was itself part of an omnibus crime bill.

The N.R.A. mobilized against the Dodd amendment; on April 9, the association sent a letter to its 900,000 members, warning that the legislation could eventually end "the private ownership of all guns." Nevertheless, the Senate approved the omnibus crime bill in May, with the gun control amendment attached.

Two months to the day after King was assassinated, Senator Kennedy was assassinated in Los Angeles. His murder further galvanized the American public behind gun control. "The only practical solution is a total ban on firearms for all but law enforcement officers," wrote one man, Alexander Markovich of Ardsley, N.Y., in a letter to The Times. A group of citizens soon formed the first major organization dedicated to gun control: the National Council for a Responsible Firearms Policy.

The Senate majority leader, Mike Mansfield of Montana, had doubts that Kennedy's assassination would prompt any further gun regulations. Then came the deluge of mail. In the week after Kennedy's death, Senator Harrison Williams, Democrat of New Jersey, received 6,000 letters advocating stronger gun laws — the most mail that he received on any matter in such a short period of time during his first nine years in the Senate. The mail for Senator Alan Bible, Democrat of Nevada, had previously opposed gun control by about nine to one; after Kennedy's death, his mail ran three to one in favor of gun regulations. By June 12, Mansfield had changed his mind and said that a measure imposing tighter gun restrictions could most likely pass the Senate.

Retailers also felt the pressure of the public. In May, Sears had already ended mail-order sales of firearms. After Kennedy's death, several other leading merchants followed suit. Some announced they would no longer carry guns or ammunition at all.

On June 24, President Johnson delivered an address on guns. He noted that the United States stood "alone among the modern nations of the world" in its lax gun laws. Johnson called for the federal registration of all firearms as well as licensing of every gun owner. Senator Warren Magnuson of Washington, a Democrat, had blocked one of Dodd's gun control bills in 1964. Now in June 1968, Magnuson told the Senate he was prepared to accept these provisions on gun registration and licensing.

But even the conversion of influential senators like Magnuson, and the groundswell of public support, couldn't protect the bill from the N.R.A. The group's supporters in the Senate, including Strom Thurmond of South Carolina (who had recently switched to the Republican Party), didn't have the strength to kill the bill, but they defeated proposals pertaining to gun registration and licensing. The final legislation, the Gun Control Act, banned interstate and mail-order sales of all firearms and ammunition; it also prohibited gun sales to felons, drug addicts and minors. In addition, it required dealers to keep records on those to whom they sold ammunition.

Johnson signed the bill on Oct. 22, 1968. But it was an uneven victory for gun control advocates. A federal committee on violence, appointed by Johnson after Robert Kennedy's death, noted that the Gun Control Act failed on the two most important scores: It neither curbed second-hand gun sales nor decreased the nation's overall arsenal of firearms.

Opinion polls continued to show that broad swaths of the public favored stricter gun regulations. But few were moved to keep the pressure on Congress for a national firearms registry or a licensure law.

The urban riots of the 1960s also sparked an increase in gun sales and ultimately helped organizations like the N.R.A., which in the 1970s set out to erode the gun control advances of the previous decade. Its head, Woodson Scott, called for a repeal of the Gun Control Act, and in 1986 President Ronald Reagan signed the Firearm Owners' Protection Act, which weakened many parts of the Gun Control Act.

The story of 1960s gun control legislation, then, is a cautionary tale. It shows that broad-based, sustained public support, combined with the heightened awareness that comes after high-profile tragedies like the King assassination and the Parkland massacre, can indeed force legislators to act. But it also shows how bursts of action are not enough, especially in the face of entrenched opposition.

For the gun control advocates who will march on Saturday, the story offers hope. But it is also a reminder that marching is only the beginning.

JASON SOKOL, an associate professor of history at the University of New Hampshire, is the author of "The Heavens Might Crack: The Death and Legacy of Martin Luther King Jr."

Do Gun Owners Want Gun Control? Yes, Some Say, Post-Parkland

BY JESS BIDGOOD | APRIL 24, 2018

TOM GALINAT, 35, a farmer and hunter who owns nine guns, traveled last month from his home in Peacham, Vt., to Montpelier, the state capital, with a firm goal in mind: Convince lawmakers to enact a ban on high-capacity magazines.

Jonathan Leach, 56, a policy analyst in Augusta, Me., and the owner of about 10 guns, testified before Maine legislators in favor of a bill to let judges order people deemed dangerous to surrender their firearms. Mr. Leach said he wanted to serve as a counterweight to gun rights enthusiasts he knew would speak against the idea.

And as thousands of demonstrators gathered in Nashville in March for student-led marches against gun violence, R. Sterling Haring, 33, a doctor and the owner of several guns including an assault-style rifle, addressed the crowd. When wounded children were flown to his hospital after a shooting at a Kentucky school in January, he said, he decided it was his duty to push for stronger gun control.

"I honestly believe that God-fearing, gun-owning Americans should be leading the debate on gun laws," Dr. Haring said in an interview on Monday, after learning of another shooting, which killed four people at a Waffle House a few miles from his house. "It just makes sense to me that if I own weapons, I should be the first one to be advocating for safety with those weapons."

As young survivors of the Parkland shooting lead efforts to tighten limits on firearms, they have met deep resistance from strong supporters of gun rights, and both sides have dug in. But the renewed national gun debate — reignited again after the shooting in the Nashville Waffle House has gotten the attention of a subset of people who are often overlooked: gun control supporters who own guns.

Tom Galinat at his home in Peacham, Vt. Mr. Galinat signed a letter to lawmakers, urging them to expand background checks for gun purchases.

Many of these gun owners will never take part in marches or make public speeches. But interviews with two dozen gun owners around the country found what polls have shown — that many of them are firm supporters of some gun control measures. In recent weeks, some have grown more vocal, holding signs at demonstrations, lobbying lawmakers or writing letters to the editor, adding their voices to those of the protesting students.

Of the 60 million to 70 million Americans who own guns, measuring how many are likely to take part in activism in favor of gun control or to change their political choices over the issue is difficult. One rough proxy for those who do not want tougher gun laws could be the five million gun owners the National Rifle Association claims as members, said Robert Spitzer, the chairman of the political science department at the State University of New York at Cortland, who has written extensively about gun policy and politics.

The N.R.A. is staunchly opposed to new gun control measures, and events following the Parkland shooting may have deepened the resolve of its supporters. In March, according to filings with the Federal Election Commission, the N.R.A. Political Victory Fund raised $2.35 million — the highest monthly amount raised for the fund in records dating back to 2003, according to an analysis by the news outlet McClatchy and verified by The New York Times. The N.R.A. did not respond to requests for comment for this story.

Only a small number of gun owners seem to be stepping forward in activism in favor of stricter gun laws, and not all agree about which laws should be toughened. But advocacy groups that support increased gun control say they sense a new kind of participation in more subtle ways, such as calls from gun owners wanting to know what the groups do, and a greater willingness to listen. The shift could also have political implications: Some gun owners said they are now paying closer attention to which political candidates receive money from the N.R.A., which takes a hard line against firearm limits.

After the Parkland shooting, Lindsey Donovan, an Army veteran in Georgia who is a member of Moms Demand Action for Gun Sense in America, said she began getting calls and inquiries from distant corners of that state, including gun shop owners in tiny towns "wanting to talk about what it is we are about." Conversations about gun restrictions with friends in the military, she said, seemed to grow more searching and less combative.

"They are not shutting me down anymore," Ms. Donovan said.

Before Parkland, her organization in Georgia had five local groups. Now there are 12. Around 1,800 people showed up to the organization's annual advocacy day in Atlanta in late February, up from 150 last year. And local chapter meetings used to draw around 30 people on any given night. Now it's often more than 100 showing up.

Dr. Spitzer said gun owners who favor gun limits reflect an often-silent middle who could be powerful allies for gun control groups.

"It's a dog that doesn't bark," he said. "It's a voice that's not heard."

ERIN SCHAFF FOR THE NEW YORK TIMES

Protesters gathered for a March for Our Lives rally in Washington in March 2018.

Long before Parkland, he said, gun owners who are not members of the N.R.A. have tended to see things differently than members. A 2009 survey by Frank Luntz, a Republican pollster, found that 30 percent of N.R.A. members supported a ban on assault weapons, compared with 47 percent of gun owners who were not members — closer to the views of the general public in such polls.

Survey data has long shown gun owners to be broadly supportive of some restrictions on firearms. Polling just after the Feb. 14 shooting in Parkland suggested a small uptick in support for stronger gun laws in gun-owning households. A poll by Quinnipiac University between Feb. 16 and 19 found that 50 percent of respondents in gun-owning households supported stricter gun laws — a figure that was seven percentage points higher than when people were asked the same question last December. In February, 97 percent of respondents in gun-owning households said they supported background checks for all gun buyers, compared with 94 percent in December. (The 1994 Brady Bill created a requirement for gun buyers to pass a background check, but the rule does not apply to private sellers online or at gun shows.)

With the N.R.A. opposed to expanding background checks, gun control groups have focused on the issue as a way to reach out to gun owners.

When the gun control advocacy organization founded by Gabrielle Giffords, the former congresswoman who in 2011 was shot in the head during an event with constituents, wanted to marshal support for a raft of proposed gun laws in Vermont, the organization worked with a local consultant, who reached out to gun owners. Before long, 61 gun owners in the state, including Mr. Galinat, had signed on to a letter to lawmakers, urging them to expand background checks.

"I'm an ardent advocate for the Second Amendment, and none of those gun safety measures threaten any of those things that I believe in," said Mr. Galinat, who also went to Montpelier for a news conference on the issue. He said his only quibble with the letter, which was written by the consultant and a local gun safety group, was that he wanted lawmakers to set even stronger gun limits.

Some gun owners said the Parkland shooting motivated them to be more vocal about their support for background checks, or about long simmering discontent with the N.R.A.

"What put me over the edge was this series of recent tragedies, both in schools and in other areas, and they just never budged," John S. Liccardi said of the N.R.A. Mr. Liccardi, 73, a hunter from Rutland, Vt., who owns several guns, stepped publicly into the gun debate for the first time in March. He denounced the N.R.A. in an op-ed for the news website VTDigger.

"If there ever is going to be any progress in sensible gun ownership and control," Mr. Liccardi said, "it has to be from the middle ground."

Some members of gun-owning families have entered the debate hesitantly. Karen Fowkes from Vienna, Va., joined a sea of people at the March for Our Lives in Washington, D.C., last month. Her husband owned a gun, she said, and she initially worried about feeling hypocritical, but joined her daughter, Colleen, at the march after some convincing.

"I said, 'Mom, this is not an anti-gun march,' " the younger Ms. Fowkes said. "I asked, 'Are you for universal background checks?' She said, 'Yes.' "

To that, the younger Ms. Fowkes told her mother, "You are for gun control, too!"

But for other gun owners, the marches had the opposite effect.

"I have a little bit more trepidation now," said Rob Mason, 47, an educational aide at a high school in Maineville, Ohio, outside Cincinnati, who owns several guns and practices shooting with his children at a range. "It seems like it's going too far."

Mr. Mason, who is not an N.R.A. member, said he supports universal background checks. But he is uncomfortable with the notion of an assault-rifle ban. His daughter, Grace, who is 16, went to a march in Ohio. He was proud she participated. But he also felt worried. The marchers' demands seemed fluid and ill-defined, raising the worry that the young people simply wanted to ban all guns.

"As a moderate, I'm like, 'Hmmm, are they really just pushing for one type of gun to be banned, or are they pushing for everything?' " Mr. Mason said. "The protesters are not talking to me. I don't think they believe that there are people like me out there."

'Almost No One Agrees With Us': For Rural Students, Gun Control Can Be a Lonely Cause

BY JACK HEALY | MAY 22, 2018

BENTON, KY. — The teenagers in rural Kentucky decided they were fed up after a 15-year-old with a handgun turned their high school into another killing ground, murdering two classmates. Like so many other students, they wrote speeches and op-ed essays calling for gun control, they painted posters and they marched on their State Capitol. The blush of activism made them feel empowered, even a little invincible.

Then came the backlash.

It started with sideways looks and laughter from other students in the hallways, they said. Friends deleted them from group chats and stopped inviting them over. On social media, people called the teenage activists "retards" and "spoiled brats," and said they should have been the ones to die during a shooting in Marshall County High School's student commons four months ago.

In a more liberal city like Parkland, Fla., or at a rally in Washington, these students might have been celebrated as young leaders. But in rural, conservative parts of the country where farm fields crackle with target practice and children grow up turkey hunting with their parents, the new wave of student activism clashes with bedrock support for gun rights.

Speaking out in a place like Marshall County, Ky., carries a price — measured in frayed friendships, arguments with parents and animosity within the same walls where classmates were gunned down.

The gulf between liberal and conservative America's responses to mass shootings was on display again in Santa Fe, Tex., population 13,000, after 10 people were killed at the high school there on Friday.

Republican leaders expressed no desire to pass gun restrictions. Many residents and students agreed with them, saying that gun control would not stop the bloodshed at America's schools.

"If we had more guns on campus with more teachers armed, we'd be a lot safer," said Layton Kelly, 17, a student who hid in a night-black classroom next to the scene of the shooting in Santa Fe.

That view resonates across rural Kentucky, where state lawmakers did not pass any new gun restrictions after the Marshall County shooting.

Most of the debate, both here in Benton, the hamlet that is home to the county high school, and at the State Capitol in Frankfort, has been focused on how to make schools more secure and how to detect potentially dangerous students. The school district in Marshall County has hired more armed officers and locked many of the high school's 86 doors. Every morning, teachers and staff members search students' backpacks and wand them with metal detectors.

The question of guns stayed largely on the sidelines.

ANDREA MORALES FOR THE NEW YORK TIMES

A billboard supporting the students of Marshall County High School in Benton, Ky. In January 2018, two students at the school were killed in a shooting.

"I don't think the Second Amendment is the issue," said Kevin Neal, Marshall County's judge/executive. "If somebody gets it in their head they're going to kill, they're going to do it."

Mr. Neal, a hulking former Marine, is a staunch gun rights supporter who said he carried a pistol on his side as he finished his lunch at JoJo's Café. He said that many adults thought the student protesters were simply "marching to march." Some parents said the students were being goaded by anti-gun groups outside Marshall County and were just seeking attention.

"They want to show, 'Look at me, look at me,' " said P. J. Thomason, whose son Case was wounded in the shooting. "Everyone that owns a gun is wrong — that's what they teach them nowadays."

Mr. Thomason said that Case survived that day because he is a competitive pistol and rifle shooter who recognized the sound of gunshots in the student commons and instantly knew to run. Case was struck in the hip, but recovered quickly and is shooting again.

"The reason he's alive is because of a gun," Mr. Thomason said.

The Marshall County students who decided to speak out for gun control said they understood the consequences of bucking the views of many of their parents, friends and neighbors on an issue as personal and emotional as guns.

"We knew we were going to get backlash," said Cloi Henke, 15, who was in a small group of students who participated in a local March for Our Lives rally one rainy day this spring.

"I just didn't think it would be so forward," said her 15-year-old friend Lily Dunn. "When people started talking about me, it knocked me down a few pegs."

It was just after school one afternoon, and Cloi, Lily and their friends — all freshmen — were squeezed into a booth at the Benton Dairy Queen. Since the shooting at Marshall, they cocoon together often, in their spot in the student commons or on a friend's willow-shaded back porch, to support each other and strategize about their tiny slice of the gun control movement.

Guns are popular in rural western Kentucky, where hunting and target shooting are common pastimes.

"Almost no one agrees with us," said Hailey Case, 16. That includes her father, who argued with Hailey after listening to her practice a speech she delivered at the local March for Our Lives rally.

One girl threatened to fight them after they held a gun control rally, they said. Letters and commenters in local news media said the students were too young to know anything.

Cloi said she had been at a friend's house one afternoon when her friend's father pulled out his AR-15 to show her "what you guys are trying to ban."

"It was kind of scary," Cloi said.

Lily, sitting next to her, said a teacher had confronted her when she came to class wearing a T-shirt in the school's orange and blue colors, showing a constellation of dots for every school in Kentucky that had been affected by a shooting.

Their own dot came on Jan. 23. According to the police and

prosecutors, Gabriel Parker, a 15-year-old student at Marshall County High, opened fire on a group of students with his stepfather's handgun as a kind of twisted social experiment, to see how people would react. Mr. Parker was arrested after he slipped out of the school among a group of students fleeing the carnage, and has been charged as an adult in the attack.

Across the country, about 60 percent of rural households own a gun — double the rate of city households — and many Marshall County students said that before the shooting they had barely thought about the gun debate. They hunted and shot air rifles at camp on Kentucky Lake, and their fathers kept handguns for protection.

Afterward, though, the gulf between their views and their parents' became impossible to ignore.

Mary Cox, 18, a senior who is involved in theater and captain of her Speech team, got into arguments with her father when he tried to buy her a compact handgun to take with her to college. One day, she said,

ANDREA MORALES FOR THE NEW YORK TIMES

From left, Hailey Case, Jordan Harrell and Lily Dunn at Jordan's home in Calvert City, Ky. The three, freshmen at Marshall County High, have been active in calling for gun restrictions since the shooting at their school.

when her father was driving her home from a rehearsal, he pressed her on her support for banning AR-15s. If she was being attacked, wouldn't she want someone with an AR-15 to come help?

"We couldn't be more opposite in what we believe," her father, Ezra, said in an interview. Still, he said, he and his wife had encouraged Mary to stay true to her beliefs.

One evening, three freshman friends who spoke at a gun control rally drove through town on their way to dinner, gliding past "Marshall Strong" signs on the Arby's and the Lake Chem Credit Union. Four months after the shooting, reminders linger everywhere. Blue-and-orange lawn signs poke up from drainage ditches. Bible verses about faith and healing are still painted onto the windows of antique shops and insurance agencies downtown.

"I don't want to see it any more," Lela Free said, staring out from a back seat.

Sitting in front in the passenger seat, Korbin Brandon, 16, thought

Hailey in an "Enough Is Enough" T-shirt.

about how his life had changed since 7:55 a.m. on that day in January.

Korbin, a freshman who speaks like a cross between Encyclopedia Brown and Alex Keaton, the conservative teenager from "Family Ties," had always thought of himself as a Second Amendment supporter and a sportsman. He'd fired a high-powered rifle when he was 8 years old.

But on Jan. 23, he was turned to face the glass walls that overlook the student commons when his classmates were being cut down.

"I saw some stuff" is how he puts it.

Though he still calls himself a conservative, Korbin decided to join the students who were organizing speeches and rallies focused on safety and gun control. When he returned to class after giving a speech that confronted the National Rifle Association, one friend yelled at him; others took a group photo without him; and a deacon at his church warned him that he sounded like a Democrat.

"They said I'd betrayed them," Korbin said of his friends. "I'd turned my back on the good way, the sportsman's way. I faced a lot of ridicule."

He was surprised at the backlash, because he does not support banning guns or accessories. But he said they should perhaps be harder to buy.

He has since tried to patch up those strained relationships, and quoted a Bible verse about avoiding foolish controversies to rebut one person who criticized him. He shrugged off the effects on him. So many other people in his hometown had suffered deeply from that terrible January day.

"There's other people that need to be taken care of," he said.

With Gun Control Nearing a Dead End, G.O.P. Turns to 'School Safety'

BY SHERYL GAY STOLBERG AND ERICA L. GREEN | MARCH 7, 2018

WASHINGTON — Republican leaders, turning away from significant gun control legislation, have shifted instead toward measures that would beef up security at the nation's schools, hoping the push will quell public uproar over the recent massacre in Parkland, Fla.

But as students and parents from Marjory Stoneman Douglas High School continue their own organizing, the school safety strategy is unlikely to end the debate. Democrats and gun control advocates accused Republicans and the National Rifle Association of using school safety to divert attention from what they see as the real issue: the proliferation of guns that have been used in mass shootings at concerts, in movie theaters, on college campuses, in churches and at workplaces, as well as at public schools.

"This time, the gun rights crowd messed with the wrong community, the wrong kids and the wrong dad," said Fred Guttenberg, whose 14-year-old daughter, Jaime, was killed at the school. He added, "I intend to be a part of breaking this gun lobby."

The Republican-controlled House plans to vote next week on the STOP School Violence Act, a bill that would authorize $50 million annually for safety improvements, including training teachers and students in how to prevent violence and developing anonymous reporting systems for threats of school violence.

The bill, drafted by Representative John Rutherford, a Republican and former sheriff from Jacksonville, Fla., is one of a flurry of bipartisan measures introduced in the House and the Senate devoted to school safety — without curbs on guns. In the Senate, a companion bill would also give schools money for physical improvements, such as installing metal detectors or bulletproof doors.

And Senator Lamar Alexander of Tennessee, the chairman of the

"This time, the gun rights crowd messed with the wrong community, the wrong kids and the wrong dad," said Fred Guttenberg, whose 14-year-old daughter, Jaime, was killed in the massacre at Marjory Stoneman Douglas High School in Florida last month.

Senate education committee, introduced his own school safety measure on Wednesday. His bill would allow 100,000 public schools to use federal dollars for school counselors, alarm systems, security cameras and crisis intervention training.

Education Secretary Betsy DeVos threw her weight behind what she said was the only approach that could muster broad support after a brief but contentious visit on Wednesday to Stoneman Douglas High School, where 17 students and faculty were gunned down on Valentine's Day.

"I think there's an opportunity to take some practical steps that many, many people agree on and continue pushing forward on things that have broad support," she said.

But as the midterm election season begins, the school safety votes may only be an opening volley.

"The Republicans would like to have the public think they're doing something and have the N.R.A. think they're doing nothing," said Representative Steny H. Hoyer of Maryland, the No. 2 Democrat in the House.

Gun control has long been one of the most divisive and contentious issues in Washington, and the rush to legislate on school safety reflects the difficulty of passing measures that have anything to do with guns. On Wednesday, students advocating gun safety legislation staged a sit-in outside the office of Senator Mitch McConnell of Kentucky, the Republican leader, chanting "Enough is enough!" and "Not one more!" Eight were arrested, police said.

But most gun safety proposals — including expanding background checks for gun purchases, raising the minimum age for buying rifles to 21 from 18, banning assault-style weapons like the AR-15 used by the gunman in Parkland and taking guns away from people deemed mentally unfit — appear to be going nowhere on Capitol Hill. President Trump's mercurial statements have not helped. At a televised White House session, he appeared to back broad gun control legislation, only to muddy his position after an evening meeting with the N.R.A.'s chief lobbyist.

One exception is the Fix NICS Act, a modest measure that would offer incentives to states and federal agencies to improve reporting to the National Instant Criminal Background Check System, or NICS, for gun purchasers. The measure, which is backed by the N.R.A., has already passed the House and has broad bipartisan support in the Senate.

But even that legislation is facing a hurdle: Mr. McConnell cannot bring it up quickly for a vote because Senate rules require unanimous consent to do so, and at least one senator, Mike Lee, Republican of Utah, has objected. And while Mr. McConnell is a co-sponsor of the Senate's version of the STOP School Violence Act, he has not said when the Senate will consider it.

The Senate's chief sponsor of the STOP School Violence Act, Senator Orrin G. Hatch, Republican of Utah, said in an interview Wednesday that his aim was to focus on "special programs and special approaches toward making these schools safer and more acceptable to the families and kids."

As for Democrats who consider the measure insufficient, Mr. Hatch said: "That's their motif every time. I mean, they know that if they can raise hell against guns and so forth, that that gives them a lot of publicity. But that doesn't necessarily help us in our educational processes."

Senator Christopher S. Murphy, Democrat of Connecticut and a co-sponsor of Mr. Hatch's bill, said he did not want the Senate to lose sight of more far-reaching legislation that would address gun violence head-on.

"That's a useful bill, but it doesn't have anything to do with gun laws," Mr. Murphy said. "Anybody whose only solution to the school shooting epidemic is to make our schools fortresses doesn't understand the root of this problem."

Randi Weingarten, the president of the American Federation of Teachers, also welcomed efforts to increase safety measures and resources, but she said legislators and Mr. Trump had used it deflect from the larger demands of the public, including students at Marjory Stoneman Douglas, who had been in the forefront of gun control advocacy since the shooting.

"The kids from Stoneman Douglas said, 'Do certain common-sense, gun violence reduction measures — don't change the subject,' " Ms. Weingarten said.

While Republicans were talking about school safety, Senate Democrats on Thursday sought to keep the focus on guns. Senators Debbie Stabenow of Michigan, and Bill Nelson of Florida convened a Democrats-only afternoon hearing to take testimony from those affected by gun violence.

Among the witnesses were Mr. Guttenberg and David Hogg, a 17-year-old Stoneman Douglas senior who has become a vocal national spokesman for gun control.

In Parkland on Wednesday, Ms. DeVos was greeted less than enthusiastically by many students, who took to social media to complain that she did not have any substantive interactions with them.

(Dwyane Wade, a basketball star for the Miami Heat who visited after Ms. DeVos, got a much warmer reception.)

"I thought she would at least give us her 'thoughts and prayers,' but she refused to even meet/speak with students. I don't understand the point of her being here," tweeted Carly Novell, editor of the student newspaper, The Eagle Eye, which covered the secretary's visit.

Another student, Aly Sheehy, tweeted, "Do something unexpected: answer our questions."

The Education Department said that Ms. DeVos visited some students and teachers and laid a wreath, and that her visit was developed with the principal's recommendations in mind to "provide minimal disruption on students' first full day back in the school." In her news conference, Ms. DeVos said she promised student journalists that she would return to meet with them.

How M.L.K.'s Death Helped Lead to Gun Control in the U.S.

BY RICHARD A. OPPEL JR. | APRIL 3, 2018

THE 1960S WERE KNOWN for their turmoil, but the degree to which guns were a factor is sometimes overlooked. Not only was a president assassinated, but an ex-Marine opened fire from an observation deck in Austin and the homicide rate leaped by more than 50 percent, driven by fatal shootings. Gun sales soared, prompted by fears of violence and rioting.

But the mayhem and violence didn't seem to move a Congress that refused to take gun-control legislation seriously. It would not even approve a proposal to outlaw the mail-order purchase of rifles, like the one Lee Harvey Oswald bought for $19.95, plus shipping and handling, and used to kill President Kennedy.

One of the few major gun control measures enacted, in California, was a reaction not to violence but to the Black Panthers' exercising their right to bear arms by patrolling with loaded rifles.

The political calculus began to change on April 4, 1968. The Rev. Dr. Martin Luther King Jr. was gunned down in Memphis. Nine weeks later, Senator Robert F. Kennedy was fatally shot in Los Angeles.

Finally, gun control became a possibility — at least in the hands of President Lyndon B. Johnson, a master at turning tragedy into legislative gain. He had used the death of President John F. Kennedy to pass the Civil Rights Act, and wrung the Voting Rights Act from the Bloody Sunday march from Selma to Montgomery. Now he would try for the Gun Control Act.

Today, it's not clear that any shooting could be awful enough to embolden Congress to thwart the National Rifle Association. But even back then, the N.R.A. throttled much of what Mr. Johnson intended to do.

"The voices that blocked these safeguards were not the voices of an aroused nation," an angry president said at the bill signing. "They were the voices of a powerful lobby, a gun lobby, that has prevailed for the moment in an election year."

He called on "those of us who are really concerned about crime" to fight for stronger laws. "We have been through a great deal of anguish these last few months and these last few years — too much anguish to forget so quickly."

The new law outlawed gun sales to felons, drug abusers, minors and those with mental illness; banned most out-of-state and mail-order gun sales; and sharply curbed imported weapons, including the cheap, tiny pistols used in many homicides.

It remains a cornerstone of federal gun law today.

The King assassination spurred the legislation not just because it horrified the nation, but also because it prompted unrest across the country, including in Washington, where lawmakers watched rioters come within blocks of the White House as thousands of federal troops were mobilized.

"It was in Congress's backyard, so they didn't have to read about it in the newspapers. They could see it," said Larry Temple, a high-ranking aide and special counsel to Mr. Johnson. "The death of Dr. King and the resulting riots in Washington had an impact on Congress and what they wound up doing."

But it wasn't until June 5, when Senator Kennedy was assassinated, that the logjam looked like it would break. A day later, a modest gun-control proposal that had languished passed Congress, raising the age to buy handguns to 21.

Still, Mr. Johnson wanted something far more sweeping. He proposed to treat guns like cars: They would be registered and their owners would be licensed.

Had something like this passed, gun-control proponents say, the United States today might look more like Britain or Australia, countries where guns are tracked and gun violence is a fraction of what it is here.

"He said, 'We have about 10 days or two weeks to get it passed,' " recalled Joseph Califano, his chief domestic adviser. " 'If we don't get it out of committee by then, the N.R.A. will kill us.' "

This time, there has been no similar urgency in Washington, even as hundreds of thousands of protesters in the capital and elsewhere have demanded changes after the killing of 17 students and staff at a high school in Parkland, Fla.

Crime is less a concern, as the murder rate has fallen sharply since the sixties. But mass shootings have become frighteningly common. Anyone — or anyone's child — could be a victim, at a school, a concert, a church, a movie theater or a nightclub.

And while a smaller percent of households own guns, the country has more of them, and they are deadlier: Semiautomatic rifles like the AR-15 have become the weapon of choice in the largest recent mass killings, leading to death tolls in the dozens.

Most people today favor tighter gun restrictions, polls indicate, just as they did a half-century ago. But the N.R.A. also wields political power disproportionate to the size of its membership, as it did then.

In 1968, the organization was not yet as uncompromising as it is today. But it used tactics that would feel familiar now.

It flooded its members with sky-is-falling warnings about the government taking away gun rights, and urged them to hound lawmakers. In a letter to 900,000 N.R.A. members in June 1968, the organization's president, Harold W. Glassen, said that the "right of sportsmen" to lawfully own and use firearms was "in the greatest jeopardy in the history of our country."

Frustrated gun-control backers called it "calculated hysteria and distortion." But it was profoundly effective.

In its coverage that month, The New York Times called the gun lobby among the most effective in Washington, citing the association's ability to get "sportsmen, farmers and gun lovers to put pressure on their congressmen."

Soon, Mr. Johnson's favored provisions were shorn from the bill by his old cadre of fellow Southern Democrats.

"Strom Thurmond is hostile as hell, and so is Jim," — James O. Eastland, Democrat of Mississippi — "and they're mutilating the bill as it is," the leader of the Senate Republicans, Everett Dirksen of Illinois, told Mr. Johnson in a recorded phone call on July 24, 1968 that is in the Mr. Johnson's presidential library. (Senator Thurmond was by then a Republican.)

The licensing and registration provisions passed neither chamber, and triumphant pro-gun forces announced it was now legislation they could "live with."

To which Representative Charles S. Joelson, Democrat of New Jersey, responded: "I suggest that tens of thousands of Americans can die with it."

The Gun Control Act was signed into law that fall.

Two years later, the N.R.A. helped defeat the re-election bid of a leading Senate proponent of tough gun laws, Joseph D. Tydings, Democrat of Maryland, a man who had won his seat just six years earlier in a landslide.

By now the N.R.A. has perfected the art of going after lawmakers who defy the organization. That is one reason the demands of mass shooting survivors and their allies, now led most visibly by the Parkland students, remain so far apart from the measures Congress is considering.

In 1956, after his house was bombed, Dr. King applied to the local sheriff for a permit to carry a concealed handgun. He was denied on the grounds that he was "unsuitable," according to Adam Winkler, the author of "Gunfight: The Battle Over the Right to Bear Arms in America."

Friends and relatives who feared for his safety urged him to hire a bodyguard and armed watchmen, he wrote in his autobiography. But soon, he and Coretta Scott King, his wife, reconsidered and gave up the one gun they owned. "How could I serve as one of the leaders of a nonviolent movement and at the same time use weapons of violence for my personal protection?" he wrote.

Fifty years ago, the death of great leaders prodded Congress to act on gun control. Now, at a similar juncture, it is the death of schoolchildren that has stirred the makings of a movement. It remains uncertain whether the current movement for gun restrictions will result in meaningful reform.

So far, the main impetus is in state legislatures. "Even in Republican-controlled states it appears there is at least some openness to doing something, building on the foundation laid over the last five years in less conservative states," said Adam Skaggs, chief counsel of the Giffords Law Center to Prevent Gun Violence. But he said Congress may not do much unless midterm elections shake things up.

For Dr. King, who would have turned 89 in January, getting rid of his gun helped him reckon with his mortality and focus on his movement.

"From that point on, I no longer needed a gun nor have I been afraid," he wrote. "Had we become distracted by the question of my safety we would have lost the moral offensive and sunk to the level of our oppressors."

This Gun Maker Wanted Safe Guns

OPINION | BY ELIZA SYDNOR ROMM | APRIL 5, 2018

IN THE EARLY 1880S, legend has it that Daniel B. Wesson, a co-founder of Smith & Wesson, the gun manufacturer, heard about a child who injured himself by cocking the hammer and pulling the trigger of one of his firm's revolvers. Wesson, known as D. B., was so distraught about the accident that he and his son, Joseph, developed a more child-safe revolver that they called the .38 Safety Hammerless.

Wesson was also my great-great-great-grandfather. Though it has been half a century since my family was involved with Smith & Wesson, I feel a twinge of responsibility every time a mass shooting occurs. I realize this is not entirely rational: I play no part in making or selling firearms and have never lost anyone close to me from gun violence. But it still haunts me.

After 17 people were killed at Marjory Stoneman Douglas High School in Parkland, Fla., I learned the shooter used a Smith & Wesson M&P 15, a version of an AR-15 military-style rifle. So I had to ask myself: What would D. B. Wesson have wanted his company to do? Would he have accepted the repeated refrain, "Guns don't kill people, people kill people"?

Obviously I cannot know what D. B. Wesson would want. But I would like to believe that he would have recoiled in horror and disbelief at the weapons created by the brand still bearing his name. And that he would have wanted all of us to ask more of his company today.

It is only fair for me, for all of us, to demand that our gun manufacturers become leaders in this national discussion around gun violence. They create products designed to kill human beings. The responsibility that must accompany the creation of weapons like an AR-15 is too large to be brushed aside by shouting about freedom and an amendment to our Constitution ratified in 1791.

Yes, the company and other gun makers have taken some steps in calling for better enforcement of the national background check system and sponsoring firearm safety programs. But they can do so much more.

I would start by asking the parent company of Smith & Wesson, American Outdoor Brands Corporation, to push for gun-violence research. Since 1996 the federal Centers for Disease Control and Prevention has been severely restricted in researching gun violence. If gun manufacturers are truly responsible organizations, they should wholeheartedly want to back this research as a public health concern. Dr. Thomas Frieden, director of the C.D.C. from 2009 to 2017, asked Congress repeatedly to fund research in gun-violence prevention but never succeeded.

In response to recent questions from BlackRock, an investment firm that owns the largest share of American Outdoor Brands, the gun maker's president, James Debney, and chairman, Barry M. Monheit, said, "We must collectively have the courage to ensure any actions are guided by data, by facts and by what will actually make us safer." Sounds like Mr. Debney, Mr. Monheit and Dr. Frieden are on the same page, so let's see Smith & Wesson lead the charge in renewing gun-violence research by the C.D.C.

I would also ask that the company publicly endorse the Brady Campaign's Gun Dealer Code of Conduct. It should support requiring universal background checks and a national registry for tracking its products, and indeed all firearms. These measures would help prevent weapons from falling into the hands of the wrong people and make it easier for law enforcement to trace guns used in illegal activities. The refrain that criminals will always get their hands on a weapon, no matter what a gun manufacturer does, is apathetic and unacceptable. What will you do to make it better?

Most obvious of all, Smith & Wesson should be pushing to require that all people who buy firearms undergo formal weapons training. Why would any responsible gun manufacturer not want a buyer trained extensively in how to properly use its very dangerous weapon?

Do more than you are doing now. Have a purpose other than making money. Take part in this national discussion. Beyond expressions of sympathy, show the families of the victims of Parkland and Newtown and Columbine and Las Vegas and every nameless gun-violence tragedy occurring every day that you care about their pain and suffering.

D. B. Wesson was a brilliant inventor who created a better gun than anyone had imagined in the 19th century. When he died in 1906, his guns had made him a multimillionaire. But he also cared deeply about the health and welfare of families and children. In his will, he left $450,000, the equivalent of more than $11 million in today's money, for a hospital specializing in homeopathic medicine that was built a few years before he died and for the construction of another hospital to provide maternity care.

If hearing about one child injured in the 1880s led him to invent the .38 Safety Hammerless, what would the more than 7,000 children killed or injured each year in the United States from gun violence stir in him? I believe if he could, he would beg the executives running Smith & Wesson today to stand up and join the fight to stop this bloodshed any way possible.

ELIZA SYDNOR ROMM, a distant relative of a co-founder of Smith & Wesson, the gun manufacturer, is a small-business owner living in North Carolina.

Glossary

advocacy Public support for a particular cause.

assault weapons A somewhat vague term to define semiautomatic rifles with a detachable magazine and pistol grip.

background check The process of looking up and storing information on individuals.

ballistic fingerprinting The examination of the unique marks that gun barrels make on bullets when they are fired.

bipartisan Involving the agreement of different groups or political parties.

bump stocks An attachment that makes a semiautomatic weapon operate as fully automatic.

caliber The internal diameter of a gun barrel.

carnage The killing of a large number of people.

concealed carry Term for laws that allow people not to display the guns they are carrying outright.

conservative A person or group that holds to traditional values and typically rejects changes to law.

epidemic A widespread disease or problem.

felons People who have been convicted of felonies, or the most serious crimes in U.S. law.

grass-roots organization A group that has been started by regular people from the ground up.

gubernatorial Relating to the governor or the governor's office.

handgun A smaller gun designed to be used by one hand; includes a pistol.

high-capacity ammunition clips A firearm magazine, or ammunition storage, that has the capacity to hold more than the typical amount of bullets.

litigation The process of taking legal action.

lobby A group of individuals who try to influence politicians for a particular cause.

loophole An ambiguity in a law or group of laws.

magazine In firearms, an ammunition storage container.

militias Groups or ordinary people who are armed and support regular military forces in the event of an emergency.

opponents Someone who competes or fights against someone or something else.

pistol A small firearm, such as a handgun, designed to be held in one hand.

registration The process of signing up for something.

rhetoric The art of persuasively speaking or writing.

Saturday Night Specials A cheap handgun that can be easily obtained.

semiautomatic A weapon that fires only one bullet at a time with a press of the trigger, then automatically reloads another bullet into the chamber.

silencer A device used to quiet the noise of a gun.

sniper rifle A high-precision and powerful weapon used by military snipers.

zealots People who are fanatical or uncompromising in following their ideals.

Media Literacy Terms

"Media literacy" refers to the ability to access, understand, critically assess and create media. The following terms are important components of media literacy, and they will help you critically engage with the articles in this title.

angle The aspect of a news story that a journalist focuses on and develops.

attribution The method by which a source is identified or by which facts and information are assigned to the person who provided them.

balance Principle of journalism that both perspectives of an argument should be presented in a fair way.

byline Name of the writer, usually placed between the headline and the story.

column A type of story that is a regular feature, often on a recurring topic, written by the same journalist, generally known as a columnist.

commentary A type of story that is an expression of opinion on recent events by a journalist generally known as a commentator.

credibility The quality of being trustworthy and believable, said of a journalistic source.

critical review A type of story that describes an event or work of art, such as a theater performance, film, concert, book, restaurant, radio or television program, exhibition or musical piece, and offers critical assessment of its quality and reception.

editorial Article of opinion or interpretation.

fake news A fictional or made-up story presented in the style of a legitimate news story, intended to deceive readers; also commonly used to criticize legitimate news because of its perspective or unfavorable coverage of a subject.

human interest story A type of story that focuses on individuals and how events or issues affect their life, generally offering a sense of relatability to the reader.

impartiality Principle of journalism that a story should not reflect a journalist's bias and should contain balance.

intention The motive or reason behind something, such as the publication of a news story.

interview story A type of story in which the facts are gathered primarily by interviewing another person or persons.

news story An article or style of expository writing that reports news, generally in a straightforward fashion and without editorial comment.

op-ed An opinion piece that reflects a prominent individual's opinion on a topic of interest.

paraphrase The summary of an individual's words, with attribution, rather than a direct quotation of the person's exact words.

quotation The use of an individual's exact words indicated by the use of quotation marks and proper attribution.

reliability The quality of being dependable and accurate, said of a journalistic source.

source The origin of the information reported in journalism.

style A distinctive use of language in writing or speech; also a news or publishing organization's rules for consistent use of language with regards to spelling, punctuation, typography and capitalization, usually regimented by a house style guide.

tone A manner of expression in writing or speech.

Media Literacy Questions

1. Identify the various sources cited in the article "Right and Left React to the Deepening Divide Over Gun Control" (on page 161). How does Anna Dubenko attribute information to each of these sources in her article? How effective are Dubenko's attributions in helping the reader identify her sources?

2. In "Support for Gun Control Seems Strong. But It May Be Softer Than It Looks" (on page 176), Margot Sanger-Katz paraphrases information from several polls. What are the strengths of the use of a paraphrase as opposed to a direct quote? What are the weaknesses?

3. Compare the headlines of "More Guns For Everyone!" (on page 107) and "The Gun and How to Control It" (on page 21). Which is a more compelling headline, and why? How could the less compelling headline be changed to better draw the reader's interest?

4. What type of story is "From One Woman's Tragedy, the Making of an Advocate" (on page 76)? Can you identify another article in this collection that is the same type of story?

5. Does Jacqueline Bennett demonstrate the journalistic principle of impartiality in her article "Towns Learn Banning Guns Is Not Easy" (on page 92)? If so, how did she do so? If not, what could she have included to make her article more impartial?

6. The article "Gun Smoke and Mirrors" (on page 164) is an example of an op-ed. Identify how Andrew Rosenthal's attitude and tone help convey his opinion on the topic.

7. Does "Do Gun Owners Want Gun Control? Yes, Some Say, Post-

Parkland" (on page 183) use multiple sources? What are the strengths of using multiple sources in a journalistic piece? What are the weaknesses of relying heavily on only one source or a few sources?

8. " 'Almost No One Agrees With Us': For Rural Students, Gun Control Can Be a Lonely Cause" (on page 190) features several photographs. What do these photographs add to the article?

9. What is the intention of the article "The Gun Lobby Is Feeling No Pain" (on page 54)? How effectively does it achieve its intended purpose?

10. Analyze the authors' reporting in "When a Gun Maker Proposed Gun Control" (on page 157) and "Once Again, Push for Gun Control Collides With Political Reality" (on page 172). Do you think one journalist is more balanced in his reporting than the other? If so, why do you think so?

11. Often, as a news story develops, a journalist's attitude toward the subject may change. Compare "Gun-Curbs Issue Revived by Dodd" (on page 11) and "Dodd Gun-Control Law Opposed by Big Rifle Group at a Hearing" (on page 42), both by Ben A. Franklin. Did new information discovered between the publication of these two articles change Franklin's perspective?

12. "A Gun Is Power, Black Panther Says" (on page 39) is an example of an interview. Can you identify skills or techniques used by Wallace Turner to gather information from Huey Newton?

13. Identify each of the sources in "How M.L.K.'s Death Helped Lead to Gun Control in the U.S." (on page 202) as a primary source or a secondary source. Evaluate the reliability and credibility of each source. How does your evaluation of each source change your perspective on this article?

14. Which article in this collection would you call a human interest story? Why?

Citations

All citations in this list are formatted according to the Modern Language Association's (MLA) style guide.

BOOK CITATION

THE NEW YORK TIMES EDITORIAL STAFF. *Gun Control*. New York: New York Times Educational Publishing, 2019.

ONLINE ARTICLE CITATIONS

APPLEBOME, PETER, AND JONATHAN WEISMAN. "Obama Invokes Newtown Dead in Pressing for New Gun Laws." *The New York Times*, 8 Apr. 2013, https://www.nytimes.com/2013/04/09/us/politics/obama-in-connecticut-to-push-for-gun-control.html.

BAKER, PETER. "Trump Says Issue Is Mental Health, Not Gun Control." *The New York Times*, 6 Nov. 2017, https://www.nytimes.com/2017/11/06/us/politics/trump-guns-mental-health.html.

BENNETT, JACQUELINE. "Towns Learn Banning Guns Is Not Easy." *The New York Times*, 12 Dec. 1999, https://www.nytimes.com/1999/12/12/nyregion/towns-learn-banning-guns-is-not-easy.html.

BENNETT, JAMES V. "The Gun and How to Control It." *The New York Times*, 25 Sept. 1966, https://timesmachine.nytimes.com/timesmachine/1966/09/25/89650417.pdf.

BIDGOOD, JESS, AND SABRINA TAVERNISE. "Do Gun Owners Want Gun Control? Yes, Some Say, Post-Parkland." *The New York Times*, 24 Apr. 2018, https://www.nytimes.com/2018/04/24/us/gun-owners-laws-parkland.html.

CLINES, FRANCIS X. "Focus of Gun-Control Fight Shifts." *The New York Times*, 7 June 1982, https://www.nytimes.com/1982/06/07/us/focus-of-gun-control-fight-shifts.html.

DUBENKO, ANNA. "Right and Left React to the Deepening Divide Over Gun Control." *The New York Times*, 22 Feb. 2018, https://www.nytimes

.com/2018/02/22/us/politics/right-left-react-gun-control.html.

FINNEY, JOHN W. "Gun Control Bill Speeded by House." *The New York Times*, 6 June 1968, https://timesmachine.nytimes.com/timesmachine/1968/06/06/77092950.pdf.

FRANKLIN, BEN A. "Dodd Gun-Control Law Opposed by Big Rifle Group at a Hearing." *The New York Times*, 20 July 1967, https://timesmachine.nytimes.com/timesmachine/1967/07/20/121587120.pdf.

FRANKLIN, BEN A. "Gun Curb Fight Opens in Capital." *The New York Times*, 9 Apr. 1967, https://timesmachine.nytimes.com/timesmachine/1967/04/09/83100714.pdf.

FRANKLIN, BEN A. "Gun-Curbs Issue Revived by Dodd." *The New York Times*, 17 Jan. 1965, https://timesmachine.nytimes.com/timesmachine/1965/01/17/98450523.pdf.

GAILEY, PHIL. "Gun-Control Advocates Are Feeling Surrounded." *The New York Times*, 27 Dec. 1981, https://www.nytimes.com/1981/12/27/weekinreview/gun-control-advocates-are-feeling-surrounded.html.

GREENHOUSE, LINDA. "Justices, Ruling 5-4, Endorse Personal Right to Own Gun." *The New York Times*, 27 June 2008, https://www.nytimes.com/2008/06/27/washington/27scotus.html.

GLABERSON, WILLIAM. "Gun Strategists Are Watching Brooklyn Case." *The New York Times*, 5 Oct. 2002, https://www.nytimes.com/2002/10/05/nyregion/gun-strategists-are-watching-brooklyn-case.html.

GLABERSON, WILLIAM. "Nation's Pain Is Renewed, and Difficult Questions Are Asked Once More." *The New York Times*, 14 Dec. 2012, https://www.nytimes.com/2012/12/15/nyregion/sandy-hook-shooting-forces-re-examination-of-tough-questions.html.

GOOTMAN, ELISSA. "Federal Bill Orders States To Give Data For Gun Sales." *The New York Times*, 9 Apr. 2002, https://www.nytimes.com/2002/04/09/nyregion/federal-bill-orders-states-to-give-data-for-gun-sales.html.

HAKIM, DANNY. "When a Gun Maker Proposed Gun Control." *The New York Times*, 9 Feb. 2018, https://www.nytimes.com/2018/02/09/business/sturm-ruger-gun-control.html.

HAN, HAHRIE. "Want Gun Control? Learn From the N.R.A.." *The New York Times*, 4 Oct. 2017, https://www.nytimes.com/2017/10/04/opinion/gun-control-nra-vegas.html.

HEALY, JACK. " 'Almost No One Agrees With Us': For Rural Students, Gun Control Can Be a Lonely Cause." *The New York Times*, 22 May 2018, https://

www.nytimes.com/2018/05/22/us/marshall-county-kentucky
-student-gun-protests.html.

HERBERS, JOHN. "Police Groups Reverse Stand and Back Controls on Pistols."
The New York Times, 27 Oct. 1985, https://www.nytimes.com/1985/10/27
/us/police-groups-reverse-stand-and-back-controls-on-pistols.html.

HERBERT, BOB. "More Guns for Everyone!" *The New York Times*, 9 May 2002,
https://www.nytimes.com/2002/05/09/opinion/more-guns-for-everyone
.html.

HERBERT, BOB. "Vital Statistics." *The New York Times*, 31 Oct. 2002, https://
www.nytimes.com/2002/10/31/opinion/vital-statistics.html.

HULSE, CARL. "Once Again, Push for Gun Control Collides With Political
Reality." *The New York Times*, 28 Feb. 2018, https://www.nytimes
.com/2018/02/28/us/politics/senate-gun-control-nra.html.

HUNTER, MARJORIE. "Gun Control Added to Civil Rights Bill By Senate, 72 to
23." *The New York Times*, 7 Mar. 1968, https://timesmachine.nytimes.com
/timesmachine/1968/03/07/77175177.pdf.

KREBS, ALBIN. "Strict Gun Control Practiced Abroad." *The New York Times*,
13 June 1968, https://timesmachine.nytimes.com/timesmachine/1968/06
/13/90034748.pdf.

KING, WAYNE. "Gun Show a Weapons Supermarket." *The New York Times*,
28 June 1985, https://www.nytimes.com/1985/06/28/us/gun-show-a
-weapons-supermarket.html.

LEWIS, NEIL A. "Statements Put White House Into a Gun Control Debate."
The New York Times, 17 Oct. 2002, https://www.nytimes.com/2002/10/17
/us/hunt-for-sniper-administration-statements-put-white-house-into-gun
-control.html.

LIPTAK, ADAM. "Revised View of 2nd Amendment Is Cited as Defense in Gun
Cases." *The New York Times*, 23 July 2002, https://www.nytimes.com/2002
/07/23/us/revised-view-of-2nd-amendment-is-cited-as-defense-in-gun
-cases.html.

LIPTAK, ADAM. "U.S. Appeals Court Upholds Limits on Assault Weapons." *The
New York Times*, 2 Dec. 2002, https://www.nytimes.com/2002/12/06/us/us
-appeals-court-upholds-limits-on-assault-weapons.html.

MARKS, PETER. "From One Woman's Tragedy, the Making of an Advocate."
The New York Times, 18 Aug. 1994, https://www.nytimes.com/1994/08/18
/nyregion/from-one-woman-s-tragedy-the-making-of-an-advocate.html.

MITCHELL, ALISON. "Politics Among Culprits in Death of Gun Control." *The

New York Times, 19 June 1999, https://www.nytimes.com/1999/06/19/us
/guns-schools-finger-pointing-politics-among-culprits-death-gun-control
.html.

THE NEW YORK TIMES. "After Vigil for Verdict, a Plea for Gun Control." *The
New York Times*, 18 Feb. 1995, https://www.nytimes.com/1995/02/18
/nyregion/after-vigil-for-verdict-a-plea-for-gun-control.html.

THE NEW YORK TIMES. "Controls on Guns Supported in Polls." *The New York
Times*, 20 June 1983, https://www.nytimes.com/1983/06/20/us/controls-on
-guns-supported-in-poll.html.

THE NEW YORK TIMES. "Drop That Gun." *The New York Times*, 24 May 1965,
https://timesmachine.nytimes.com/timesmachine/1965/05/24/101549827
.pdf.

THE NEW YORK TIMES. "A Gun Control Moment." *The New York Times*, 28 Apr.
1999, https://www.nytimes.com/1999/04/28/opinion/a-gun-control
-moment.html.

THE NEW YORK TIMES. "Rethinking Ballistic Fingerprints." *The New York
Times*, 11 Nov. 2002, https://www.nytimes.com/2002/11/11/opinion
/rethinking-ballistic-fingerprints.html.

OPPEL, RICHARD A., JR. "How M.L.K.'s Death Helped Lead to Gun Control in
the U.S." *The New York Times*, 3 Apr. 2018, https://www.nytimes
.com/2018/04/03/us/martin-luther-king-1968-gun-control-act.html.

QIU, LINDA. "Republican and Democratic Lawmakers Get Facts Wrong on Gun
Policy." *The New York Times*, 1 Mar. 2018, https://www.nytimes
.com/2018/03/01/us/fact-check-gun-meeting-trump-congress.html.

ROBINSON, DOUGLAS. "Gun Curbs Backed by a Rifle Expert." *The New York
Times*, 26 Apr. 1967, https://timesmachine.nytimes.com/timesmachine
/1967/08/26/90396689.pdf.

ROMM, ELIZA SYDNOR. "This Gun Maker Wanted Safe Guns." *The New York
Times*, 5 Apr. 2018, https://www.nytimes.com/2018/04/05/opinion/gun
-maker-safe-guns.html.

ROSENTHAL, ANDREW. "Gun Smoke and Mirrors." *The New York Times*, 27 Feb.
2018, https://www.nytimes.com/2018/02/27/opinion/guns-age-limit
-mental-hospitals.html.

SANGER-KATZ, MARGOT. "Support for Gun Control Seems Strong. But It May Be
Softer Than It Looks." *The New York Times*, 24 Mar. 2018, https://www
.nytimes.com/2018/03/24/upshot/gun-control-polling-student-march
-parkland.html.

SEELYE, KATHARINE Q. "Democrats, Using Finesse, Try to Neutralize the Gun Lobby's Muscle." *The New York Times*, 10 Sept. 2002, https://www.nytimes.com/2002/09/10/us/democrats-using-finesse-try-to-neutralize-the-gun-lobby-s-muscle.html.

SEELYE, KATHARINE Q. "Killings May Not Affect Gun Control Measures." *The New York Times*, 20 Oct. 2002, https://www.nytimes.com/2002/10/20/us/a-hunt-for-a-sniper-the-gun-lobby-killings-may-not-affect-gun-control-measures.html.

SEMPLE, ROBERT B., JR. "President Asserts Texas Shooting Points Up Need for a Law." *The New York Times*, 3 Aug. 1966, https://timesmachine.nytimes.com/timesmachine/1966/08/03/82866956.pdf.

SHERRILL, ROBERT. "The Gun Lobby Is Feeling No Pain." *The New York Times*, 11 Apr. 1971, https://timesmachine.nytimes.com/timesmachine/1971/04/11/82002204.pdf.

SOKOL, JASON. "America Passed Gun Control in 1968. Can It Happen Again?" *The New York Times*, 22 Mar. 2018, https://www.nytimes.com/2018/03/22/opinion/gun-control-1968.html.

SPITZER, ROBERT J. "America Used to Be Good at Gun Control. What Happened?" *The New York Times*, 13 Oct. 2017, https://www.nytimes.com/2017/10/03/opinion/automatic-weapons-laws.html.

STOLBERG, SHERYL GAY, AND TIFFANY HSU. "Republicans Open to Banning 'Bump Stocks' Used in Massacre." *The New York Times*, 4 Oct. 2017, https://www.nytimes.com/2017/10/04/us/politics/bump-stock-fire-legal-republicans-congress.html.

STOUT, DAVID. "Bush, Usually Opponent of Gun Control, Backs 2 Restrictions Proposed in Congress." *The New York Times*, 28 Aug. 1999, https://www.nytimes.com/1999/08/28/us/bush-usually-opponent-of-gun-control-backs-2-restrictions-proposed-in-congress.html.

TURNER, WALLACE. "A Gun Is Power, Black Panther Says." *The New York Times*, 21 May 1967, https://timesmachine.nytimes.com/timesmachine/1967/05/21/113435974.pdf.

Index

This book is current up until the time of printing. For the most up-to-date reporting, visit www.nytimes.com.